The Work Revolution

Jonathan Males, PhD

First published February 2024
by Spiramus Press Ltd
102 Blandford Street
London W1U 8AG

www.spiramus.com
© Jonathan Males

ISBN
9781913507503 Paperback
9781913507510 Digital

British Library Cataloguing-in-Publication Data.

A catalogue record for this book is available from the British Library.

The right of Jonathan Males to be identified as the author of this work has been asserted by him in accordance with the Copyright, Designs and Patents Act, 1988.

Printed and bound in Great Britain by Grosvenor Group, Essex

The Work Revolution

Performance and Leadership in the Modern World

Endorsements for

The Work Revolution

Performance and Leadership In the Modern World

The Work Revolution is as essential reading as *The 7 Habits of Highly Effective People.*

Darren Fergus, President of Tweidpharma

The Work Revolution is optimistic, practical and a warm companion to support and encourage us to bring our best selves to our work, our purpose and our lives.

Hetty Einzig, author of *The Future of Coaching: Vision, Leadership and Responsibility in a Transforming World*

Jonathan Males shares a lifetime of experience in sport and business to create a manual for modern leaders to be better humans.

Matt Horton, Chief Strategy and Innovation Officer, Aztec Group.

Bursting with wisdom and insight, this is an enjoyable and accessible read. This is a book to pick up again and again when you need a leadership 'pick me up'.

Alison Barnes, CEO, New Forest National Park Authority

This is very pragmatic and builds useful frameworks and exercises for busy executives.

Bev Cunningham, Chief People Officer, Ricoh Europe.

Contents

My story ix

Acknowledgements x

About this book xi

Introduction...xiii
    How we got in this mess xiv
    A vision of healthy high performance xvi
    The ART of performance xviii

Chapter 1. Who are you and what do you want? 2
    Summary 2
    Who are you? Personality and character... 2
    What do you want? Motivation and thinking styles 5
    Light and dark 7
    Healthy, sustainable motivation 11
    Conclusion.. 14
    Want to know more? 14

Chapter 2. Worldviews – our inner maps of the world........................... 16
    Summary 16
    The match between your worldview and the demands of your role 20
    Transitioning from one worldview to the next 21
    Communication between worldviews 23
    Conclusion.. 25
    Want to know more? 25

Chapter 3. Self-awareness as the key to change 27
    Summary 27
    Map of inner experience.. 28
    Immunity to change 32
    Enabling change 35
    The power of 1% 38
    Conclusion.. 39
    Want to know more? 39

Chapter 4. Think straight 42
    Summary 42
    Why thinking matters 42
    How working life distorts thinking – and how our thinking distorts working life
    43
    Cognitive biases – inbuilt thinking problems 45
    The perils of short cuts – how assumptions can get in the way 46
    How to improve the quality of your thinking.. 48

Thinking with others 53
Conclusion... 53
Want to work on this? 54
Want to learn more?.. 54

Chapter 5. Relate well **56**
Summary 56
Why relationships matter 56
How modern work and our minds distort relationships........... 57
Self-awareness 58
Self and other... 59
Understanding needs in relationships 62
How to improve relationships... 65
High performance communication 69
Giving feedback – understanding impact and intent............... 73
Conclusion... 76
Want to work on this? 76
Want to learn more?.. 76

Chapter 6. Act powerfully **78**
Summary 78
Why action matters 78
Why modern work stops us getting much done 79
Organising your working environment 81
The creative orientation – overcoming barriers to action 83
Structural tension 84
Friction 85
Mindfulness and current reality – accepting what is 86
Bringing this to life 87
Alignment, purpose and motivation 89
Conclusion... 91
Want to work on this? 91
Want to know more? 91

Chapter 7. Building Exceptional Teams **94**
Summary 94
Why teams matter 94
How teams are changing.. 95
Harnessing the power of teams 97
Being an effective team member....................................... 99
A framework for exceptional teams 101
The outcomes – belief, confidence, and trust 109
The Five Cs 110
Remote and hybrid teams.. 111

Conclusion.. 113
Want to work on this? 113
Want to know more? 113

Chapter 8. Leading in new worlds **115**
Summary 115
What sort of world are we living in?... 115
Cynefin – a map for new worlds 117
Given the VUCA world in which we live, what does leadership mean and what do leaders need to do? 120
We don't need another hero 122
New archetypes for leadership – hearth holders and agitators, coaches and explorers 123
Your inner readiness to lead 123
Look out for the shadow 124
People and task: coach and explorer 125
Stability and change: hearth holder and agitator 128
The relationship between the archetypes 130
Meaningful purpose.. 131
Reimagining the future 132
Conclusion.. 136
Want to work on this? 137
Want to know more? 137

Epilogue – the power of having enough, rather than always wanting more **139**

Bibliography **142**

THE WORK REVOLUTION

My story

I grew up in Tasmania in the 1960s and 70s, an adopted child in a culture where self-esteem was based more on sporting prowess than academic achievement. Not being particularly skilled on the football pitch, I sought a sport I was good at, and was fortunate to discover white-water kayaking. At this time it was still possible to explore wilderness rivers no-one else had ever kayaked before. This fed my thirst for adventure, yet I was still drawn to competition, and I followed my ambitions as a slalom racer, achieving success at a national level and racing internationally on the Australian team at four world championships through the 1980s. Travelling and competing on the slalom circuit for ten years was a rewarding and highly challenging experience that sparked my curiosity about performance psychology. In 1987 I decided that I wanted to be a performance psychologist and work to help people reach their potential in sport and business – a decision that has shaped my life and career ever since.

Following my first slalom career and a degree in psychology, I coached the Australian slalom team at the 1992 Barcelona Olympics, and then moved to Britain where I developed a dual track career in sport and business. I have worked as a sport psychologist with talented athletes and coaches to help them prepare for Olympic and Paralympic competition through the last seven Games. After I completed a PhD in the psychology of high performance, I wrote my first book, "In the Flow" in 2014 as a sport psychology guide for paddlers and coaches in kayaking. Alongside my colleagues at Mezzana Partners, I work as an executive and team coach with business leaders in the UK and beyond. I live in London and have four adult daughters, who teach me much about life. Whitewater remains a passion, and I continue to enjoy slalom competition and travel.

Acknowledgements

I have worked alongside and learned from many talented people who have generously shared their experience and insights. I hope some of what I have learned from them rubs off on others too.

Christopher Connolly and the late John Syer were ahead of their time in developing teams and I still use what I learned from them thirty years ago. Karen Ellis, Sol Davidson, Julie Allen and Brian Chandler helped me to understand the nature of organisations and dig deep into human nature. Working alongside Nic Whitfeld has been a source of fun and much learning. Chris Taylor and the Actionable community showed me how new habits can power behaviour change. William Winstone hugely contributed to developing the ART of Performance framework, and Katherine Bond was pivotal in shaping our model of Exceptional Teams. I'm very fortunate to have them both as friends and business partners today.

Claire Males helped to ensure that my claims are well referenced. Carl Upsall and Cecilia Hallpike from Spiramus have done a wonderful job turning a word document into a proper book – thanks both of you.

Alistair Mant was a significant influence in my understanding of leadership and systems thinking. As fellow Australians living in Britain, we shared something of an outsider's perspective on politics and culture. He passed away during the Covid pandemic and I greatly miss his wisdom, grace and humour. This book is for you Alistair.

About this book

This book is designed to help you become more effective *and* more human at work and at home. It is a combination of curation and creation, and I hope I have acknowledged the many sources I draw upon, as well as being clear when I am offering my own ideas. I have only included material that has proved its benefit with real people doing real jobs. Each short chapter begins with a bullet point summary – the Twitter/X version for those with short attention spans. Then there is the body of the chapter, in which I use the same language and level of detail I use with my coaching clients, which seems to suit busy people who aren't academic psychologists. If you are an academic, you might find this approach lightweight, but this book wasn't written for you. If you want to know more, I end each chapter with recommended further reading and there are additional notes for key references.

Introduction. The way we work is f***ed

I begin with a deliberately provocative picture of the world of work because for many people, being at work is often stressful and at worst toxic. This is a natural consequence of pursuing endless growth, which has been a distinctly mixed blessing. Many of us are better off than ever before, but this has come at great cost to society and the natural world. Fortunately, we're not powerless and we can each play a role in creating more meaningful ways of doing business. I call this healthy high performance because wellbeing and performance at work can be complementary, not mutually exclusive.

Section 1. Foundations

Chapter 1 Who are you and what do you want?
Chapter 2 Worldviews – our inner maps.
Chapter 3 Awareness brings change.

Consider this first section a human being's user guide, intended to provide a working understanding of what makes us who we are, what shapes our view of the world, and how we change and grow. Just as it is perfectly possible to drive a car without knowing what happens under the bonnet, you may want to go straight to Section 2 for practical tools and techniques. But, if like me you prefer to know a bit about the inner workings (of cars and people) then read this section first.

Section 2. The ART of Performance

Chapter 4 Think straight.
Chapter 5 Relate well.
Chapter 6 Act powerfully.

Healthy, sustained performance relies on your capacity to think, relate and act. Skilfully combining all three is an art that you can develop and refine, playing to your natural strengths and balancing out weaknesses. This section offers a chapter devoted to each capability, showing why it is important, and what you can do to develop. I suggest specific new habits that will help you sustain consistent change. If you are already clear about the area you want to focus on, feel free to dive into the relevant chapter.

Section 3. Putting this into practice

Chapter 7 Building exceptional teams.
Chapter 8 Leading in new worlds.

Healthy high performance isn't just about you as an individual. In this section I will show how the principles apply in two related domains. First, when we come together in teams. I believe that teams are the most powerful vehicle for changing how we work, and in turn to change an organisation's culture to make it more humane. Then, I examine your role as a leader with responsibility for the performance of other people and whole organisations, focusing on how this requires a move from single-handed, heroic leadership to a more collaborative approach. I will introduce four new leadership archetypes for today's challenges: coach, hearth holder, agitator and explorer.

Epilogue. The power of enough

I conclude with an invitation to move from always needing more (the siren call of modern capitalism) to instead seeking only to have enough. Enough what? Enough love, enough security, enough control in our individual lives and enough fresh water, healthy food, shelter and meaningful work for the world.

Introduction

The way we work is f***ed

We live and work in a socioeconomic system that was breaking down even before the 2020 pandemic. The tenets of 'neoliberalism' – cheap credit, limited financial regulation, low wages, off-shoring – may have contributed to an overall increase in prosperity in recent decades,[1] but they have also created greater social inequality,[2] and led to massive environmental damage. Austerity and the gutting of public services in the UK has caused misery, lowering life expectations without reducing national debt.[3,4,5] Our economic system now serves the needs only of a minority, and the rise of reactionary, populist political leaders is just one response to this failure. The pandemic and a rising awareness of a climate emergency adds to a sense of anxiety as more and more people realise that we are not heading towards a future of shared future prosperity and a liveable planet. Driven by short term profit and survival, the natural consequence is that many businesses have become stressful, and at worst, toxic, places to work. The same is true of high-performance sport. The pressure to win at any cost has led to drug abuse, bullying by coaches, and unethical behaviour.[6] Many of us live and work in an environment that, at some level, feels threatening.

This description may sound over the top, but I come face-to-face with the consequences through my work as an executive coach. My clients work in a range of businesses such as commercial property, pharmaceuticals, investment management firms, and local authorities to name a few. Despite the differences in their professions, they face common challenges. All work long hours – the notion of a '40-hour week' is fanciful and 50 – 60 hours is the norm. All are swamped by daily demands, in the form of several hundred emails and back-to-back virtual meetings that often leave no time to even eat or drink through the day. Those working in the public sector face a relentless challenge to do more with less and suffer chronic stress as a result. Working from home has made this worse for many who struggle to maintain a healthy boundary between family and work, and end each day exhausted by 'Zoom fatigue.' Despite holding leadership roles that carry a big salary and notionally at least, authority, I work with many people who feel powerless in the face of corporate expectations, government policies and unrealistic targets. Most have given up hope of returning to 'business as usual' and recognise that the VUCA world of *volatility, uncertainty, complexity*, and *ambiguity*[7] is the new normal. Reaching the limits of their influence and energy, they are decent people who want to do a good job, grow their career and look after their families. Many are aware that there is more to life than work – and they are starting to ask bigger questions of themselves, and their companies. The so-called 'great resignation' may well be one response, as those with the means to work less choose to do so.

If you recognise this description of working life, I want to help you to redefine what it means to perform and thrive in your roles at work and home. We need to start by understanding how we got in this mess, so bear with me for a brief canter through the last six hundred years of history.

How we got in this mess

The period from the 1400s to the late 1770s was the time of the European enlightenment, a blossoming of culture and exploration that saw Europeans begin to explore, trade and colonialize Africa, the Americas, and Asia. The Christian religion was a strong moral and political force – and was co-opted by monarchs and traders to justify their expansion. It was mutually convenient to spread the word of God to 'heathens' while taking their gold and colonizing their lands. The slave trade between Africa, the Americas and Europe created great wealth for the English and Dutch merchants who arranged the ships and bought and sold enslaved people, spices, tobacco and cotton. But it was risky too, and joint stock companies (the forerunners of today's corporations) were invented to mitigate and spread the financial risks of traders. Financial institutions like the Bank of England and Lloyds of London[8] can trace their origins to this period – all based on financing the activities and protecting the profits of merchants drawing their wealth from international trade with Europe's colonies.

The late 1770s marked a remarkable historical inflection point. Within a few years the French Revolution took place, the US Declaration of Independence was signed, James Watts invented the steam engine and Scottish philosopher Adam Smith published his famous work *The Wealth of Nations* in 1776, that articulated the principles and philosophy of the free market, where the most important component in creating wealth was labour. He also wrote a companion book, *A Theory of Moral Sentiments* which hoped a harmonious and moral world would emerge, but this has sadly been less influential.[9] The 19th century saw accelerated wealth creation using coal powered steam engines in English mills and factories that span cotton grown and harvested by African enslaved people who had been transported by force to the United States. The reality of Smith's vision of capitalism grew, as it became possible to generate, reinvest and grow wealth based on the labour of others.[10] Emigration from Europe to the 'new world' across the Atlantic fuelled the population growth and wealth of the

United States which had abundant land and natural resources (at the cost of conflict with the indigenous population). American innovation boomed, and the industrial world's centre of gravity moved from Britain to the United States. By the 1920s, capitalists like John D Rockefeller became billionaires through companies like Standard Oil and Henry Ford revolutionised car factories through production lines. Frederick Taylor took efficiency to new limits through his ideas of scientific management, strictly controlling and measuring the activities of workers, ensuring labour translated to capital.

Sociologist Max Weber coined the term the "Protestant work ethic" in 1904 to describe the prevailing attitudes that he saw as the underpinnings of capitalism: success, in this world and the next, came to disciplined, frugal individuals who worked and prayed hard.[11] Yet capitalism grew not just from individual effort and beliefs. It also emerged because of cultural and social forces, as Martin Luther King wrote:

"We have deluded ourselves into believing the myth that capitalism grew and prospered out of the Protestant ethic of hard work and sacrifice. The fact is that capitalism was built on the exploitation and suffering of black slaves and continues to thrive on the exploitation of the poor — both black and white, here and abroad." [12]

The end of the Second World War marked another inflection point. The United States emerged as the dominant world power, based on the strength of its natural resources and industries. Germany and Japan quickly sought to rebuild their societies and industries in the same free-market image, actively supported by billions of dollars invested through the Marshall Plan. The USA's capitalist venture was challenged by the second biggest power to emerge from the War, the Soviet Union, and the Cold War between the two powers followed. Some would see the next 30 years as the high point of the free market with increasing prosperity and living standards driven by an increasingly global marketplace – and indeed the fall of the Berlin Wall in 1989 seemed to indicate that 'the west had won.' But all was about to change yet again.

The same year the Iron Curtain came crashing down, an English computer scientist called Tim Berners-Lee invented the World Wide Web. The digital age began in earnest, triggering a profound change in the way we live, work and make money. The fundamental basis of the capitalist economy shifted from cheap labour to exploiting tangible resources to controlling data.[13] The interconnectivity of people, markets and information exploded, as did the complexity of the financial world and the application of 'free market' neo-liberalist ideology to everything from education to healthcare and public services. This house of cards crashed in 2008, brought down by a combination of deregulation, cheap credit and greed-fuelled risk taking.[14] Since the great financial crash, we have seen more overt criticisms and challenges to the prevailing capitalist worldview – from political movements like Occupy Wall Street, Extinction Rebellion and even Pope Francis. All have questioned the primacy of a system based on unregulated capitalism and the pursuit of profit at all costs, and argued instead for a more holistic approach that recognises the ecology in which we live. Yet, phoenix-like, capitalism has grown back after the crash looking remarkably unchanged.

I suggest we can draw out some key assumptions of the capitalist world view. These assumptions are based on interpretations of Christianity which portrayed mankind as separate from, and superior to, the natural world. Also on a distorted application of Adam Smith's philosophy that emphasised the individual, while ignoring what he said about the importance of moral society, and by the limitations of human psychology when it is driven by fear and greed. These implicit assumptions include:

- That financial value is more important than human, social, or natural value.
- That the aim of business is the never-ending growth in financial value.
- That individual self-interest is the most powerful social and economic driving force.
- That people are 'resources' to be maximised.
- That mankind is separate from and somehow superior to the natural world.
- That the natural world has no implicit value other than as a source of financial profit.
- That 'the market' is always the most rational and efficient way of allocating resources.

With these underlying principles driving our society and ways of working, is it any wonder we find ourselves in the mess we are in?

A vision of healthy high performance

Thankfully, a new approach to business, society and the planet is emerging that is based on values of collaboration, tolerance, fairness, equality and a much bigger answer to the question "who is my neighbour?" This means opening to the realisation that we are all neighbours sharing the one planet, and our fates and fortunes are inextricably linked regardless of our local or national identity. Known as "conscious capitalism",[15] I hope this can lead to more sustainable businesses that make wise use of resources and treat colleagues, customers, and the natural world with dignity. The breakdown of neo-liberalism is a painful process and there are no guarantees of a fast or easy transition to something better. But I have hope and optimism that we can each play a part in getting there.

Given this context, it is a fair challenge to ask what any one of us can do alone. Many of us feel overwhelmed and anxious when considering the world's problems, and respond by either pretending nothing is wrong, or else polarising to cynicism or hopelessness. I believe that business leaders have a key role to play in bringing about positive change because leaders "cast a long shadow" and their thoughts, relationships and actions can influence many people within and beyond their immediate circle.[16] Not just their employees and team members, also through their customers and suppliers. I want to help leaders learn to be more compassionate, more effective, and more capable of establishing honest and productive relationships at work and in their families to create positive ripples throughout our companies and beyond. By working with the grain of human nature, not against it, we can develop more meaningful ways of doing business, so that wellbeing and performance at work and in life are complementary, not mutually exclusive. I call this approach *healthy high performance.*

How do we do this? There are three key aspects of healthy high performance – how we think, relate and act. These are inter-related; because how I think influences how I act and relate, and my behaviour and relationships will influence how I think. I consider these separately for the sake of simplicity, and I call this framework the ART of Performance (logically the sequence think, relate, then act makes more sense, but the TRA of Performance isn't so catchy).

THINK
I am fundamentally optimistic about human nature. I believe we are each capable of emotional, psychological and spiritual growth that increases our choice, wisdom and compassion. Equally, we are all capable of being narrow-minded and engaging in negative and damaging behaviour towards ourselves and others. This happens because the human mind reacts to perceived threats by seeking

out evidence that justifies our own beliefs, so we tend to live in 'echo chambers' that bounce back confirmatory messages.[17]

Healthy high performance requires the capacity to manage your brain's natural tendency to close down under threat, and instead stay open to different perspectives. This requires the courage to test your assumptions and ask; "how might I be wrong?"

RELATE

Personal insecurities and profit-focused working practices means that all too often we objectify colleagues, customers and stakeholders and lose sight of our common humanity. Healthy and effective relationships lie at the heart of healthy high performance. These relationships are based on empathy, appreciation of differences and mutual trust. This requires self-awareness and the capacity to see people as people, not resources or problems.[18]

ACT

The heavy demands and information overload of today's digital workplace leads all too often to feeling threatened and overwhelmed.[19] Our inbuilt survival strategy of fight, flight or freeze[20] leads to two unhealthy responses: procrastination and distraction (freeze and flight) or compulsive overwork (fight). Neither are sustainable, and both contribute to toxic environments and personal suffering. The healthy high performance alternative is to manage these habitual responses and instead make clear and constructive choices about actions that will lead to real outcomes.

The ART of performance

By learning how to optimise and balance our abilities to act, relate and think we can create the conditions for sustained and healthy high performance. Purposeful engagement flows from people working together in trusting relationships aligned to a common goal. Informed action arises when we think clearly and manage our time and energy. Creativity comes by constructively working with others to test and develop ideas. If we can learn to bring the best of ourselves to our work, I'm optimistic we can create the conditions for people to thrive. And by doing so, we can each play our role in the work revolution.

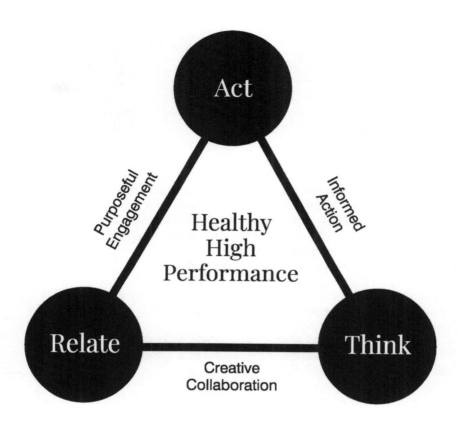

[1] *Our World in Data* (2020).

[2] *Our World in Data* (2023).

[3] Mattheys, K., Warren, J. and Bambra, C. (2018).

[4] Further discussion of the impact of austerity on living standards can be found at the Institute of Health Equity, (2020), *The Marmot Review, Ten Years On*, available at https://www.instituteofhealthequity.org/resources-reports/marmot-review-10-years-on

[5] *Office for National Statistics* (2022), Government debt data, available at https://www.ons.gov.uk/economy/governmentpublicsectorandtaxes/publicspending/bulletins/ukgovernmentdebtanddeficitforeurostatmaast/march2022

[6] Examples of unethical culture and abuse in sport evidenced in the *Whyte Review into Gymnastics* (2022), Accessed from https://www.sportengland.org/guidance-and-support/safeguarding/whyte-review

[7] Bennett, N. and Lemoine, G. J. (2014).

[8] Kynaston, D. (2020).

[9] Adam Smith's life and work is discussed by Jesse Norman, who argued that Smith was more concerned with the human cost of the free market than people remember. See Norman, J. (2019). Also see Smith, A. (1776). and Smith, A. (1812).

[10] For a discussion of Smith and Weber in the context of capitalism see Tutino, J. (2017). and Barbalet, J. (2008).

[11] Weber, M. (2012).

[12] King, M L. (1967).

[13] Mason, P. (2016).

[14] Reserve Bank of Australia, (2018). *Explainer for the 2008 Financial Crisis*, https://www.rba.gov.au/education/resources/explainers/the-global-financial-crisis.html

[15] For a discussion of "Conscious Capitalism", see Mackey, J. and Sisodia, R. (2013).

[16] For an example of the broader emotional impact of leadership, see Goleman, D. et al (2001).

[17] Nickerson, R. S. (1998).

[18] For more examples of how businesses can focus on people, see Warner, C. T. (2016)

[19] Discussion of the impact of technology see Rock, D. (2009), Greenfield, S. (2014) and Ritchel, M. (2010)

[20] Donahue, J.J. (2020).

Section 1. Foundations

These three chapters offer a working understanding of what makes us who we are, what shapes our view of the world, and how we change and grow. I will introduce several psychological frameworks and theories that I use to guide my work as a performance psychologist and executive coach. I often share these principles with my clients because they help them understand their own behaviour and how to change it. I know some readers are not naturally drawn to theories, so I have brought these ideas to life through a range of characters. Each character is a composite of real people with whom I have worked, and I will bring them in at various stages of the book to illustrate what it looks, sounds, and feels like to develop and apply the ART of healthy high performance.

Chapter 1. Who are you and what do you want?

Read this chapter if you would like to understand more about 'what makes people tick', how your personality and character have formed and how this might influence you now. If you work with other people, it will help you understand them better too. You may already have a good understanding of yourself, or you might just want to solve a pressing problem – if so, move ahead to Section 2 where there are plenty of practical tips.

Summary

- We all have core psychological needs; for control, for acceptance, and for security.
- The ego is the function of the mind that seeks to meet these needs.
- Motivation is the drive to meet these needs or protect against losing them.
- Everyone develops strategies to meet their psychological needs.
- These strategies are influenced by and, in turn, influence your personality.
- These strategies shape your own behaviour and expectations of others to perform.
- Strategies usually work for a while then become limiting.
- Healthy performance requires growing beyond ego motivation to a develop higher order motivation and constructive, growth-oriented strategies.

Who are you? Personality and character

Who are you and what do you want? There is the 30 second answer you leave as a voicemail message, and a much longer answer that unfolds over a lifetime. Psychologists have developed many theories that attempt to explain personality and motivation, and what follows is not an exhaustive critique of a large and contested academic field. It is my working model, one that I have found pragmatic and useful to help people make sense of who they are (personality and character) and what they want (motivation). It is important to differentiate between which aspects are open to change, and which tend to be stable over the course of your life. If you understand this difference, you can take a realistic approach to improving your performance, by knowing when and how to play to your strengths and when and how to change and grow. And if you are a leader or manager responsible for others, then this chapter will be just as useful to help you understand what makes other people tick.

Let's begin by understanding what aspects are relatively stable over your life. This is usually described as your personality. The growing academic consensus is that personality is due in roughly equal proportions to the interaction between your genes and your environment, and it can be best understood by five core traits. Each of these traits are like the slider controls on an old-fashioned graphic equaliser. There is a continuous range from low to high, and each of us has a point on the scale that is our most typical way of being. While some personality models break these traits down into their component parts, we will stick the 'big five' known by the acronym OCEAN:

Big 5 Trait	Low	High
Openness	*Practical, conventional, risk averse, prefers familiar experiences.*	*Creative, imaginative, artistic, prefers new experiences.*
Conscientiousness	*Spontaneous, careless, impulsive, lacks focus.*	*Organised, careful, attention to detail, self-controlled.*
Extraversion	*Quiet, reserved, aloof, contemplative, stoical.*	*Outgoing, talkative, like attention, attuned to positive emotions.*
Agreeableness	*Uncooperative, hostile, non-compliant, difficultly relating to others.*	*Trusting, friendly, empathic, cooperative, easily relates to others.*
Neuroticism	*Emotionally stable, not easily stressed.*	*Prone to worry, anxious, sensitive. Attuned to negative emotions.*

Does being high or low in a personality dimension mean that you always behave this way? No, because our behaviour is always a function of the situation, our personality, and our learned responses. It simply means that you are more likely to demonstrate this type of behaviour at any given time, and that you will seek out, or avoid, situations that match your personality preference. Traits are generally stable over time, and change, if it happens, occurs slowly. To illustrate this, I score low on the Conscientiousness scale, and this shows up positively because I can be adaptable and stay relaxed when things go wrong. Less helpfully, it also contributes to a lack of attention to detail. I know I need to pay extra attention if I am filling in a form, and there are some tasks I simply do not do or delegate if I can. This characteristic was first brought home to me as a 12-year-old, and still bedevils me 48 years later:

Don't forget me

For many years I kept a small, shrivelled potato hanging on a string. Carved into it were the words "Don't forget me." As a 12-year-old, my first leadership experience came as the Patrol Leader in the 1st Lindisfarne Scout troop, competing for the Clark Trophy, a state-wide competition comprising a weekend of scouting and bushcraft tasks. Our patrol finished second by a single point. Although this was the best result our troop had ever achieved, it was hugely disappointing not to win. At our next meeting, our Scout Leader, Ray 'Skip' Christie, presented each of us with a small memento, reminding us of how we each could have won the extra points we needed. My potato referred to my oversight in not including potatoes in a roast lamb meal we cooked over an open fire. It was a powerful lesson in shared responsibility – we would have won had any one of us made a tiny improvement. And it was the first (but sadly not the last) time my lack of attention to detail had significant consequences.

There are many questionnaires that will help you understand your personality, such as the Lumina Spark Portrait[1] and the Hogan Personality Inventory.[2] Knowing about, appreciating, and working with your basic character is important. It also helps you to tease out other, more malleable aspects of 'who you are and what you want'.

If personality has strong genetic influences and is relatively stable, what else contributes to who we are? And is it open to change? To answer these questions, we first need to understand a little about motivation.

What do you want? Motivation and thinking styles

The word motivation derives from the Latin word *movere*, to move. To move requires energy and intent. Where does this energy come from? Why are some people driven by ambition whilst others seem happy to let their lives unfold as they will?

The answer is that we are driven not by one singular force, but by a combination of many, often competing needs; to earn enough money to pay the bills, to get promoted, to be a respected professional, to invent something clever, to solve a big problem, or to save the world. Some are more motivated by what they do outside of work – pursuing a sport or hobby or caring for their family. Often there are less virtuous forces at play too; the need to avoid looking stupid, to gain others' approval, to bolster fragile self-esteem, to prove others wrong.

I find it helpful to start with a working premise that everyone shares three basic psychological needs; a need for control, a need for acceptance, and a need for security. There are other human needs too, like achievement, fun, creativity, contribution and meaning. But for now, we will focus on control, acceptance, and security because they are particularly relevant when we are young. The ego, a term introduced into psychology by Sigmund Freud to refer to 'the self',[3] is the function within the mind that is responsible for meeting these psychological needs, and hence ensuring our safety and survival. The ego often gets a bad press – "he is all ego" or "she is driven by ego", or more radically "you must overcome your ego". But the reality is that the ego's function is essential to shape our identity and enable action in the world. It is impossible to be a well-functioning human without a well-functioning ego.

How then do these basic psychological needs show up, and how do they influence adult motivation? The answers start early. Infants are biologically 'hard-wired' to bond with their parents to secure their physical survival needs of food and nurture. A baby cries when they are hungry or uncomfortable, signalling an unmet need, a behaviour designed to provoke a parent into action. As children get older, they come to realise that they depend on adults for more than food and a clean nappy. Adults, especially parents, are the source of psychological well-being too. They can provide a child with control, the sense of agency and ability to influence; with acceptance, experienced as love and affirmation; and with security, the feeling of certainty and predictability about what will happen in the future.

There is no such thing as a 'perfect' environment in which children feel all these psychological needs are totally and absolutely fulfilled. As a result, children (or at least their emerging egos) creatively respond to real or perceived deficits in these core needs and strive to meet them.

Some deficits are very real and can cause immense damage. Consider the tragedy of the children who grew up in Romanian orphanages during the rule of the dictator Nicolae Ceauşescu.[4] These children lacked human contact and suffered terrible physical and psychological neglect. As adults they have suffered emotional and psychiatric problems and are unable to form meaningful relationships. Fortunately, few of us grow up in such an extremely toxic environment. A more typical pattern is the discovery that certain types of behaviour lead to our parents or caregivers providing affirmation, attention, and approval. Because this behaviour is adaptive to our psychological security, it is reinforced. Other types of behaviour do not reliably lead to our basic needs being met, so these behaviours will fade away. These behavioural patterns are also shaped by our inherited personality traits. For example, if I have inherited a tendency to be extraverted and agreeable, my motivational strategies may well focus on relating well with others and developing strong friendships.

Likewise, a child growing up in an unpredictable, chaotic family, perhaps with an absent parent, may come to discover that taking charge is a reliable way of feeling more secure. The strategy of taking charge is reinforced and becomes more prevalent as part of the child's character. Depending on the inherited personality, this leads eventually to adult behaviour that may be strongly controlling (if the underlying trait of neuroticism is high) or perhaps more positively authoritative (if the underlying trait of neuroticism is low). A typical experience of high achievers is receiving praise and parental attention for academic success. Their ego learns to associate good marks at school with parental attention that meets the basic need for acceptance and so this strategy is reinforced. This develops into a drive to succeed and achieve high standards.[5]

Paradoxically, it is often those parents who withhold some aspect of basic needs who create the strongest 'motivation' in their children. This is because the ego is motivated most strongly by the *fear* of not having a basic need met. I have come to learn that people who are 'highly motivated' and 'high achievers' are often driven more by fear than aspiration. This may sound somewhat pessimistic but having worked closely with hundreds of people in business and sport I have heard and seen many life stories that illustrate the point. A powerful example can be found in Olympic cycling gold medallist Victoria Pendleton's autobiography. She describes how her intense motivation to succeed on a bike was driven by her desire for her father's approval.

> "It's taken my whole life to reach this point (the 2008 Olympic final). The little girl trying desperately to stay in sight of her dad, pedalling up a hill until it seemed her heart might burst, would not believe we'd end up here. There were no Olympic dreams then. That small girl, me in a different world, just wanted Dad to slow down or look back to see I was all right... I just want Dad to love me, and be proud of me, and so this is where I've ended up."[6]

Within each of us, the ego striving to gain or avoid losing security, acceptance and control combines with inherited personality traits in a rich, complex, and often contradictory motivational blend, with different strategies coming to the fore in different parts of our lives. Some strategies fit a socially accepted 'success narrative' – work hard at school, get a job, get married, start a family and work for forty years to pay off a mortgage. Other strategies are not so constructive or well-accepted – like joining a street gang to gain status and acceptance by peers. And some strategies may be constructive yet challenge social norms – like dropping out of a well-paid medical career to work in war zones with *Médecins Sans Frontières*. The blend that anyone develops will be shaped by inherited characteristics, by their early family experience, and by their social context.

It is important to recognise our personality traits and seek to work with the grain of our character, not against it. These traits will shape the motivational strategies we develop, which then impact how we get on in the world. Let's take a closer look at what this means.

Light and dark

I have outlined how the ego's drive to meet the basic needs of security, acceptance and control lead to a range of strategies that become part of a person's thinking and behaviour.

Here are four typical strategies, illustrated by a simplified composite example of real people with whom I have worked. I want to show how the ego driven strategy has both helped, and eventually hindered, each person's effectiveness and happiness. The ego can certainly drive performance – but it cannot sustain it. See if you can identify what basic needs are at play in each of these stories.

Laura
Laura is an ambitious lawyer in her early thirties. The older of two children, she grew up in a stable middle-class family with parents who valued education and set high expectations. She is bright and worked hard at grammar school to achieve stellar results that propelled her seamlessly through a law degree at a top university and into a prestigious law firm. This demanding environment requires and rewards hard work and attention to detail. Laura puts in long hours to produce high quality work and has been identified as a potential partner.

Laura is, by many standards, successful. Yet within the safety of a coaching relationship, she reveals the tensions she feels. Her drive to be perfect both helps and hinders. It helps because she is gaining a valuable reputation as a safe pair of hands amongst clients and the partnership. It hinders because it comes at the cost of her family life – she is in work by 7.00 am and rarely gets home before 9.30 pm every day, so time with her husband is short and marked by exhaustion. She worries about the risks of making a mistake and letting down her boss, she worries about letting down her husband and failing at her marriage, and she feels torn between her desire to become a partner in the firm and her desire to become a mother. She is caught in a toxic bind between standing out and fitting in. Her life strategy has been to be a 'good girl' and to gain approval through conformity and academic success. She has never really failed at anything, and the thought of doing so now is terrifying.

James
James was born in a poor part of Wales. As the middle child of three, he remembers that there was never enough to go around, and life was tough. His mother did her best to hold the family together, but his dad was an inconsistent figure who had his own demons, found mainly at the bottom of a bottle. Despite this challenging beginning, James was the first in his family to go to university, and he later discovered he had the right combination of commercial savvy and charm to become a successful property developer. Now in his mid-forties, he leads a successful company employing nearly twenty people.

THE WORK REVOLUTION

Like Laura, James' life appears successful, if you judge it by his Ferrari, his Caribbean holidays and his six-figure income. Less successful is the experience of James' team, who live in fear of his infamous 'table thumping' responses to bad news or mistakes. Less satisfying too is his family life. His first marriage ended in divorce and his teenage children are not backward in expressing their resentment at his younger second wife. He sleeps poorly and is often irritable at work. James cannot understand why he never feels like he has made enough money no matter how much profit his company makes. His energy and drive are remarkable, but the personal costs are adding up.

Amir

Amir grew up in a close and loving family, and with a little embarrassment admits having been the 'apple of his mother's eye', the boy who could do no wrong. He recalls his early family life to have been happy, idyllic even, with no memories of particular hardships or difficulties. Arguments were rare, and it was always considered bad manners to bring up disagreements or criticise others – far better to keep the peace.

His career began in sales, and he quickly developed a reputation for being highly likeable and building strong relationships with his clients. Nothing was ever too much trouble for Amir, and he would do whatever it took to ensure his clients were happy. Amir has just been promoted to manage the sales department of his company and he is discovering some new challenges. As a manager, he now has a wider range of responsibilities. It is no longer enough to keep his own clients happy, he now needs to manage his team and ensure they meet their sales targets. He is finding this tough, especially with a couple of team members who are under-performing. He is happy to offer praise and encouragement but is terrified at the idea of criticising or challenging others. One team member, Harriet, is a challenge because she is defensive about her underperformance and hasn't responded to Amir's somewhat tentative attempts at constructive feedback. As a result, Amir now avoids contact with Harriet wherever possible. Amir's career blossomed based on him being a 'nice guy', yet this characteristic is now starting to limit his ability to manage and hold his team to account.

Anne

Anne is in her mid-forties and is a senior manager in a local authority. Anne's mother was a teacher, her father a church minister, and she grew up in a home that valued contribution and service above material aspirations. She began her career as a social worker, dealing with a wide range of people living in difficult and challenging circumstances. Her steady demeanour, empathy and problem-solving skills led her to progress to a team leader then on to management roles, and she now leads the whole authority's children's services. It is a complex, demanding and often thankless role that she throws herself into whole-heartedly, working 70-hour weeks, attending evening community and council meetings and trying to stretch her team's limited resources to cure unlimited problems and suffering. She finds it almost impossible to switch off, and despite her own 'front line' social work experience her team is finding her demands are becoming unreasonable.

Chris

Chris is the CEO of a global engineering firm of 6000 people. He grew up on a farm where he was expected to (literally) muck in from a young age. This gave him a strong work ethic and a practical attitude to life. He studied engineering at university then joined a multi-national as a graduate trainee, beginning a varied career in which he worked his way up the ladder in a succession of management roles that increased his span of responsibility and took him around the world. His company took development seriously, so over the years he has been exposed to a range of formal training ranging from an MBA to an intensive four-week leadership retreat. Three years ago, he was head-hunted by a competitor to turn around its business. He enjoys his job, especially now his three children have grown up and his frequent travel creates less of an issue at home. He figures he has another two years left, by which time he will have pretty much delivered on the strategy to re-position the company, and then he will be ready for a new challenge. He is not sure what that will be, but it probably won't be sitting on beach or walking around a golf course. Instead, he is increasingly intrigued by the work of a conservation organisation that is preserving wildlife habitats in Africa.

As you read these examples, perhaps you are starting to notice similar patterns in your own life, or in the behaviour of people with whom you live and work. Perhaps you can see a little of yourself in each of the stories –

or nothing at all. Laura, James, Amir, Chris and Anne's circumstances and life stories are unique to them but they each illustrate common life paths. Ego driven motivation is like the rocket fuel that blasts a spaceship free of earth's gravity into space. It helps us get going early in life and propels us into adulthood. Yet at some point a spaceship runs out of conventional fuel and needs an alternative source of energy that will sustain its journey. If we are born into the right circumstances, encounter good role models and opportunities at the right time, or are simply blessed with some luck, we can find ourselves doing all right in life. Not everyone suffers great trauma as a child! But most of us will encounter the uncomfortable realisation that our ego driven strategies undermine our ability to live a healthy and sustainable life. This realisation can be a valuable jolt that leads us to explore and develop new sources of meaning and motivation.

Paradoxically, many people do not want to let go of ego-based motivation because they worry that they will 'lose their edge' or will change 'who they really are'. This is natural because although painful at times, their strategy has worked for them up to now. Fortunately, the opposite is true. Far from losing who we are, examining what drives us leads to discovering new capacities and freedoms, even to discover more about who we really are. Let me use a different analogy to explain why this is so. Imagine you are driving along a motorway, trying to keep up with the traffic. Your foot is heavy on the accelerator, the engine is revving hard but you are not going any faster. Other cars seem to go past with ease. You look down at the gearshift and realise you are in third gear, so you change up to fourth and then fifth gear to liberate the engine's power and go faster with less effort. Fear-based motivations are like third gear – useful for getting up to speed but ultimately inefficient and limiting. Developing new strategies, learning a new story about yourself, and tapping into a more constructive motivation is like adding new gears that allow the engine to transfer to its power to the road more efficiently.

Healthy, sustainable motivation

Up to now we have focused on survival needs – gaining security, acceptance, and control. Psychologists have long recognised that once these needs are met, people start to seek more from life.[7] These higher order needs include learning, growth, creativity, purpose and meaning. Often, these drives do not emerge until later in life, when we have established a secure base in the world. The famous psychologist Carl Jung even suggested that living from these higher order needs defined the second half of life.[8] My sense is that higher order needs are appearing earlier for more people than in the past, at least in the more prosperous parts of the world. Perhaps because the overall standard of living has increased, and material needs are more easily met, younger people are now seeking more from work and life.[9]

Let's take a closer look at higher order needs to understand how they hold the key to healthy and sustainable performance. One of the most useful tools for assessing the balance of ego driven and higher order motivation is the Learning Styles Inventory (LSI) developed by Human Synergistics.[10] I have adapted the LSI constructive thinking styles in the following descriptions.

ACHIEVEMENT
The drive to achieve is central to being human, but it has two very different expressions. Ego driven aspiration creates a form of competitiveness that is defined by comparisons with others, which means that I judge my success and self-worth by whether I have beaten the opposition or have a more expensive car than my neighbour. Psychologists call this extrinsic motivation and contrast it with intrinsic motivation, which is defined by challenging yourself to be the best you can be according to your own standards. This inner drive to excel leads to robust and enduring motivation, demonstrated by sporting champions like Roger Federer who continued to set themselves new goals, despite having won many titles and achieved great wealth. Mature achievement also seeks real outcomes that make a meaningful difference – producing a tangible result, product or service for others, not just 'ticking the box'.

LEARNING
A key facet of intrinsic motivation is a hunger for learning and a desire to grow – a process Abraham Maslow termed self-actualisation.[11] How else can I continue to achieve unless I learn and grow? Learning is enabled by a sense of optimism and the curiosity to seek out new challenges. It requires humility and openness to feedback. Carol Dweck's work on a growth mindset[12] has shown how these characteristics support greater resilience and creativity too. Learning fast is critical to adapt to change and without it, people, teams, and whole organisations stagnate and become toxic.

CREATIVITY

Creativity comes from a combination of the needs to achieve, the desire to learn and the capacity to play – sparking one of humanity's most precious gifts, the ability to invent and innovate. Whether creativity leads to a new line of computer code, a new melody, or a new anti-biotic, it demonstrates our capacity to adapt and evolve in the face of new challenges. Creativity adds positive energy and fun to an environment, providing a necessary contrast to the hard grind of serious endeavours.

DEVELOPING OTHERS

As we move beyond the ego's self-centeredness, it is natural to pay more attention to the growth of others and to gain satisfaction and pleasure from teaching, coaching and mentoring. This might happen professionally, by supervising a new member of staff, or outside of work by coaching a junior football team. Some see this as a way of ensuring they leave a legacy, of passing on their skills and experience so that others can benefit. The generosity to develop others is a powerful marker of a healthy and high performing culture.

RELATIONSHIPS

Rather than other people simply being a source of security or validation, we can start to see them as real human beings who have their own needs, hopes and dreams. This awareness opens the possibility of real contact and the experience of different, and deeper, relationships. Such relationships provide a rich source of learning, support and enjoyment and can add enormous benefit to workplaces and families. Paradoxically, a more mature approach to relationships can also lead to difficult conversations because it brings the courage to address, rather than avoid, other people's damaging or problematic behaviour. I like the term carefrontation to describe the constructive process of being caring, yet direct, within a mature relationship.

SEEING A BIGGER WORLD

An often-quoted African proverb says that it takes a village to raise a child. While some critics challenge that it only takes a family, I believe this proverb still makes an important point. Yes, families are essential, and they form the foundation for much of our effectiveness as individuals and lie at the heart of the social fabric.

Yet building a wider network of relationships does not diminish the family's importance, it simply places it in a larger context. Sustainable, healthy performance requires that we understand and appreciate our role in the wider world, not live in an echo chamber. One client who really understood the power of communities convinced his firm to sponsor a local youth charity, which led to highly paid lawyers discovering the reality of poor families living less than 200 metres from their shiny office tower block. This did a wonderful job at tempering the lawyer's behaviour each year at bonus time and increasing their willingness to contribute pro-bono to worthwhile causes.

Conclusion

In this chapter I have given a working model of how our character and identity is shaped by a combination of inherited and largely stable personality traits, and the subsequent motivational strategies and thinking styles that are layered on this foundation. Whilst we all respond to the ego's survival needs, it is only by exploring higher order motivations that we start to build the thinking and behaviours that will support a sustainable approach to life that underpins healthy high performance. In the next chapter we add an important, but poorly recognised, aspect of human growth and identity. This is the role of the evolving worldviews that shape how we make sense of ourselves and our lives.

Want to know more?

For an accessible guide to personality and the OCEAN model, read *Personality – what makes you the way you are.* Daniel Nettle (Oxford University Press, 2009).

To understand more about the trap of striving for perfectionism, see *Happy Ever After – escaping the myth of the perfect life.* Paul Dolan (Allen Lane, 2019).

A practical application of Human Synergistics thinking styles to leadership can be found in *Leadership transformed, how ordinary managers become extraordinary leaders.* Peter Fuda (Profile Books, 2014).

---

[1] Lumina Spark (2023), Lumina Learning LTD, see:

https://luminalearning.com/products/lumina-spark/

[2] Hogan Assessments (2023) see:
https://www.hoganassessments.com/assessment/hogan-personality-inventory/

[3] Freud's original work on the Ego can be found in his paper the Ego and the Id, Freud, S. (2011). For contemporary discussion on how the Ego appears in popular culture see Lunbeck, E. et al, (2019).

[4] For a discussion of the impact of neglect in the Romanian context, see Weir, K. (2014).

[5] Nettle, D. (2009).

[6] Pendleton, V. (2012), p 3.

[7] Ryan, R. M., Deci, E. L. (2018).

[8] For a more detailed exploration of this theme, see Hollis, J. (2003).

[9] Weeks, K. (2019).

[10] For more detail on this see the Human Synergistics Website available at
https://www.humansynergistics.com/about-us/the-circumplex

[11] An accessible guide to Maslow's theory can be found here:
https://simplypsychology.org/maslow.html

[12] Dweck, C. (2016).

Chapter 2. Worldviews – our inner maps of the world

Have you ever been in a conversation where people seem to completely 'miss' each other's meaning? Despite speaking the same language each seems to be understanding the topic in a completely different way. Puzzling and often frustrating especially if you're one of the people involved. This chapter will give you new ways to make sense of this and similar challenges, which are often nothing to do with personality, intelligence, or education – instead, this can be all about the worldviews each person holds.

Summary

- Worldviews are overarching frames of reference that shape our meaning, identity and action.
- We grow through a series of worldviews through our whole life.
- They evolve over time and go through recognisable stages.
- Worldviews shape our ability to respond to our working role and life challenges.
- Understanding worldviews helps to navigate your own behaviour and interaction with others.
- Transitions between worldviews can be confusing to yourself and others.
- Worldviews are open to change through constructive destabilisation – a combination of challenging experiences and appropriate support.

As well as understanding that your personality is largely stable and inherited and that your thinking styles are shaped by the ego's survival drive, there is another important aspect of the human condition that we need to understand. This is the discovery, made by different researchers in the fields of psychology and adult development, and long known in a range of wisdom traditions, that adults can grow through a recognisable series of stages over a lifetime. This body of knowledge goes under the rather off-putting title of *adult constructive-developmental theory*[1] and these stages are variously called 'developmental frames', 'operating systems' 'forms of mind' or 'action logics' but I am going to use the term 'worldview'. Like the old saying that a goldfish is the last to know about water, your worldview may not even be visible to you. It is your taken for granted understanding of yourself, the people around you, and the way things are. You look at life *through* your worldview, and rarely look *at* your worldview itself. Worldviews are like a secret code that can explain many issues in life, whether these are misunderstandings between people, why we grow dissatisfied with jobs that were once fulfilling, or struggle to adapt to a new role.

When you were a young child, your worldview was basic. You were self-centred and events were good or bad, right or wrong. As you matured, you started to gain a more nuanced sense of the world, taking more perspectives into account. You started to understand that other people saw things differently and that right and wrong aren't always clear cut, that sometimes 'it depends'. Over time you have gained access to new worldviews and eventually even stopped using early maps altogether. It is likely that as an adult, you will have access to two or three worldviews, with one representing your 'centre of gravity' at any given time.

Let's look at the six most common worldviews that you will find in the world of work, typically held by people from their early twenties to early sixties.[2] I am going to ask Amir, Laura, James, Anne and Chris to each describe themselves from the inside out to try to give a sense of what it is like to inhabit each worldview. As you read each description, notice which aspects you recognise in yourself and in others. It is unlikely that you will identify yourself entirely within one description, but you may well notice that one worldview is most familiar to you now.

Conformist: Amir

I like feeling accepted by my team and it's important that I fit in with them. I keep things simple – I just aim to keep my customers happy, so that keeps my boss happy too and life is good. I don't think about deep stuff, or worry about other parts of the business, or think much about the future. My appearance is important to me, and I make sure I wear the right brands and styles of clothing – which are the same ones my friends wear. I don't like conflict and will tend to stay quiet and keep my head down if there is a disagreement. Life is pretty straightforward, so long as I stick with my group and do what I know.

Expert: Laura

I am really proud to be a professional and work at my firm and to have achieved so much in my career so soon. It is important to me that I do my job properly and I believe there is always a right way to do anything. That's what being a lawyer is all about. When I am uncertain, I refer to my boss and to the rules to work out what to do. I get impatient with people who don't understand why this is important, or who want to do things their way. I like working with other lawyers so long as I respect their competence. I am not particularly interested in other parts of the firm, and to be honest I don't really think too much about what my clients do, so long as I get their contracts right and follow the letter of the law. I prefer to get on with my job, and I don't have much time for 'navel gazing'. I am generally not comfortable with feedback, especially from people who do not understand what I do. I find it hard to delegate my work, because deep down I don't really believe my team will do the job properly, or as well as I can myself.

The conformist and expert worldviews are marked by what Harvard psychologist Robert Kegan calls the 'socialised mind'. This means that the main frames of reference are external and drawn from the morals, narratives, and expectations of our social context. He suggests that in the next worldview we begin the move to a 'self-authored mind', in which we start to choose the values that we want to use a guide and begin to question the assumptions and rules we have grown up with so far.[3]

Achiever: James

I define myself largely in terms of the results my business achieves, through my efforts and through the team. I am learning to step back from the detail and look at the bigger picture, although it is still easy to get drawn into a problem when it is in my area of speciality. I have learnt that there is 'more than one way to skin a cat' and I am willing to learn about new ways of working that can help me, or my part of the business, be more effective. As a result, I am generally open to feedback on how I am doing. When people don't think the same as me or start behaving like a 'jobsworth' I get annoyed. I pride myself on being a rational thinker who can step through a problem logically to find a good solution. I often find myself playing a co-ordinating role, getting different people with a range of skills together to work as a team. I am starting to get quite interested in 'what makes people tick' and I am drawn to personality models that give me clear categories that describe different types of people. I have a clear sense of my own values and priorities in life, that I am willing to stand by.

Taken together, the expert and achiever worldviews cover most people at work. The growth of the self-authored mind reaches its peak with the next worldview. At this stage we have a powerful realisation that everything is relative and open to individual interpretation.

Individualist: Anne

I see the world, and the people in it, as complex with many different moving parts. Life is not as straightforward as I believed when I was young, and I am starting to question basic premises that I once took for granted. Like the idea that people's position in life is due to how hard they work or whether they did well at school. Improving the lives of troubled families is a real challenge and there are no simple solutions, so many different factors interact like education, individual attitudes, unemployment, changes in work opportunities, medical care... Despite all this I am increasingly fascinated by my own inner world of thoughts and feelings, of understanding how my history has shaped who I am now, of the patterns to my behaviour. At times this all seems a bit overwhelming. I am noticing that often I will make connections and worry about issues that my colleagues do not even seem to see, which gets frustrating because these things are so obvious to me. At best I am seen as creative and as 'thinking out of the box', but at worst I am told to just keep things simple and stop complicating things.

The final worldview we are considering is relatively rare at work, because it often does not emerge until people are in their mid-forties if at all. It is a useful frame of reference for people working in more senior or complex roles. Kegan describes this worldview as representing the 'self-transforming mind' because it brings the capacity to see systemic patterns and shades of grey, not simply black and white, and therefore to find common ground among apparent differences.

Strategist: Chris

I have reached a good place in life, and I am comfortable in my own skin. I have acquired a lot of experience over the years, working my way through different jobs in varied parts of the world that have tested and stretched me along the way. I know my strengths and I am confident enough to be open about my vulnerabilities too because that's how I keep learning and growing. I appreciate that people are different because of their own unique histories and circumstances. I can mostly be tolerant of people who are very different from me – although I can get angry if my people do not follow our core values, and then try to defend themselves rather than be open about their own behaviour. My job is to manage the dynamics between the many different interests that make up our business – I have to pay attention to our shareholders and market forces, manage relationships with our key clients, keep my senior team aligned and focused at the right level, then stay connected with the people on the rig teams and ops directors. I am pretty agile at taking different perspectives and can think my way around a problem using a range of different approaches – combining logic and intuition. I can deal well with complexity and ambiguity, largely because I have learned how to manage my own anxieties and fears so that I can keep a clear perspective on both the long term and the immediate problem. Our industry is changing too, and we will need to adapt even more in the future – and I don't know how ready our people are for that.

There are three ways in which worldviews are important to healthy high performance; the match between your worldview and your work role, transitioning between worldviews, and communication between people with different worldviews.

The match between your worldview and the demands of your role

One common criticism I hear of adult developmental theory is that it is hierarchical, with the implicit judgement that some worldviews are 'better' than others. I disagree with this for two reasons. First, your worldview says nothing about your skills, experience, competence, personality, or motivational strategies. All of these are relevant to your quality of life and performance. Second, there is no guarantee that later worldviews will lead to any more happiness than earlier ones – later worldviews simply offer a more expansive map. The most important comparison is not between one worldview and another, but between a person's available worldviews and the demands they face in their life at that time. A good fit provides a useful foundation for effective performance, a mismatch creates a problem or an opportunity depending on the available support.

For example, I have a friend 'Mike' who works as a machinist, each day crafting highly specialised parts out of brass, gold and steel for very expensive shotguns. He has spent over thirty years working for the same niche company, honing his skills and experience. He has no interest to 'climb the ladder' to become a manager and gets intense satisfaction from producing exquisite, unique work. My sense is that he operates largely from the expert worldview, and he lives a fulfilling life, enjoying his work, time with his family, and his sporting pursuits on the weekends.

By contrast, I once worked with 'Phil', who also operated from the expert worldview. He led a small team who oversaw the application of engineering safety standards. Trained as an engineer, he had many years of field experience, he knew and understood the legislation and how it needed to be applied. The challenges and demands of this role were matched well by his worldview. Things changed after he was promoted to a Head Office role, where he was responsible for shaping and defining new policies and influencing legislation. This was a much more ambiguous situation, that exposed him to competing interests and political dynamics that he had never encountered before. The challenges of this role required a more complex mental map, perhaps even that of a strategist. He lacked confidence in the new role, became anxious, and struggled to make meaningful progress. He suffered stress and was signed off work for several weeks. Once he and his boss understood the situation, he moved back to a technical role which he happily resumed. Could he have been helped to grow into the new role? Possibly, and moving to a new role can be a powerful catalyst for growth when the gap is not so great.

You may feel this is a version of the *Peter Principle*, the management dictum that people rise in an organisation to their level of incompetence. In a way it is, with the proviso that I am talking about more than competence. Acquiring new skills – to play the piano, to create a spreadsheet, to ask good questions or to write a business plan, brings competence and confidence to your professional and personal roles. But acquiring technical skills does not necessarily require, or invoke, a change in the way you make sense of yourself or the world around you.

Transitioning from one worldview to the next

In times of increasing volatility, uncertainty, ambiguity and complexity, simply acquiring new technical skills will be necessary but insufficient to thrive. You may also need to gain access to new worldviews, a process sometimes called vertical learning.

Development through the different worldviews is natural as we mature through life and adapt to different contexts and challenges. It is an adaptive response to increasingly complex environments. Each of you will experience a unique journey, at a pace shaped by your own nature and your outer experience. Some of you may spend a significant portion of your working life within one or two worldviews, others may move at a faster pace. Sometimes you may get 'snagged' and spend more time using a more limited map than is ideal. People vary greatly in the pace of this growth, and how far along the journey they get. It seems that growth can be stalled by several factors – particularly by early or unresolved psychological trauma, and by a constrained and unstimulating environment. Conversely, growth is fostered by exposure to new and different experiences, challenges, and cultures, and by being stretched enough to learn but not to break. This is sometimes called 'constructive destabilisation' because it relies on the right combination of experiences in which you are metaphorically 'in over your head' but with enough support to learn how to swim.

I want to focus on the impact of the two key transitions that are most relevant in a working context, the move from expert to achiever, and from achiever to individualist.

EXPERT TO ACHIEVER
In a working context, a very common worldview transition occurs when someone goes from being a subject matter expert, reliant on applying hard-earned knowledge, solving problems, and often working in a relatively narrow field, to fully inhabit the role of a manager. A manager's role requires taking a longer time frame, the ability to co-ordinate a range of people and processes, and a focus on achieving outcomes. This is an easily recognised, but at times rocky journey. Not everyone wants to take on a managerial role (remember Mike happy in his workshop) and you will all have your examples of people promoted too soon or beyond their capacity (Phil, struggling in a policy role). An important part of the process is to learn to value and gain satisfaction from new activities, as well as to learn to let go of the satisfaction gained from aspects of your old role.[4] In the early stages of the transition, it can be tough to feel like you are no longer 'hands on' and applying your hard-won technical skills. You may even question what value you are adding if you are 'only' managing others. With patience, curiosity and the right support, your new map will take shape.

ACHIEVER TO INDIVIDUALIST

The transition between achiever and individualist feels very different, because it represents a shift in centre of gravity moving fully into Kegan's self-authored form of mind, leaving behind the influence of the socialised mind. This means that it can feel quite confusing and un-settling, alongside which many people start to enter this phase around their forties, a time well known for the classic 'mid-life crisis'. Not all such 'mid-life' crises are linked to the transition from achiever to individualist worldviews, but it is not unusual for them to coincide. It can be especially useful to work with a coach at this time, to help make sense of the changes and discover that rather than a 'break-down' you might be experiencing a 'break-through.' Once normalised, I have seen many people start to enjoy the liberation and freedom that can come with a move into the individualist worldview.

Communication between worldviews

Because worldviews are invisible, even to yourself, and are still not commonly understood, you may not fully appreciate the impact they have on effective communication. How many times have you heard the following sorts of complaints – or indeed voiced them yourself?

Rob, a maths teacher, says:

> *"I am so fed up with our new head teacher. She's not even a maths teacher and she doesn't understand the methods I am teaching the kids. She just bangs on about outcomes and targets, which are a distraction to me and a total waste of time."*

Sue, the head teacher, says:

> *"Rob's a lovely bloke and very passionate about his subject. He really wants to do the right thing for his kids, but he just does not understand that as a school we have bigger responsibilities. Unless we can prove our progress and achievement our funding suffers."*

Rob is speaking from a typical expert worldview, which lends itself to the aspects of his job in which he works independently within his mathematics class. Sue views her role from an achiever perspective, equipping her well for the challenging demands of managing a whole school and its stakeholders. Both Rob and Sue care deeply that their students get a good quality of education, but their perspectives and priorities are shaped by their roles and the worldviews they hold, leading to friction and misunderstanding.

Myriam, an internal change consultant in an oil and gas company, says:

> *"The engineers see everything as black and white; they just want the simplest way to get from A to B. They do not understand that things aren't always so simple, and we can create more problems than we solve if we just charge ahead."*

Rick, a senior engineer working with Myriam says:

> *"She is always thinking conceptually, and she doesn't always apply it so well. I sometimes have difficulty following her train of thought because it is hard to see the relevance."*

Myriam sits across Achiever and Individualist worldviews and so the capacity to see interdependencies comes easily to her, and she assumes (wrongly) that her colleagues will appreciate the benefit. Instead, she often confuses her colleagues, who more typically work from an expert worldview. This is the prevailing worldview in their company, especially amongst the people responsible for operations.

Appreciating your own, and others' worldviews, can make it much easier to manage misunderstanding and reduce friction. Without this awareness, it is all too easy to blame friction on personality differences or incompetence. Once you start to get curious about your own, and other's worldviews, whole new possibilities for collaboration and understanding start to emerge. Each worldview brings certain aspects of reality into focus, and a healthy organisation recognises and values the contributions each worldview can make, so long as there is a good match between the role demands and the capacities of the person fulfilling it. The conformist worldview brings a sense of belonging and connection, expert brings deep knowledge and expertise, achiever co-ordinates and manages, individualist challenges and questions the status quo, while strategist underpins mature leadership.

Conclusion

A healthy high performing working environment will provide a home for all relevant worldviews and utilise their strengths. It will also foster learning, not just of new skills but to enable the natural process of growth and evolution. Robert Kegan and his colleagues call this a DDO, a Deliberately Developmental Organisation, one that:

> *"creates immersive cultures for continuous individual growth as the necessary means of achieving superior business results."*

This ties beautifully with higher order motivation that we introduced in the previous chapter. Kegan says:

> *"A DDO is organized around the deceptively simple but radical conviction that organisations will best prosper when they are deeply aligned with people's strongest motive, which is to grow."*[5]

By creating the conditions for people to grow, in a way that aligns with creating valuable products or services, it is possible to build sustainable and thriving organisations. Surely, this gives us hope for reducing the level of frustration and disengagement so many people feel at work today?

In the next chapter, we will take a closer look at the mechanisms for growth and change, focusing on the critical role of self-awareness.

Want to know more?

For practical and accessible applications of adult constructive development theory, look online for talks by Jennifer Garvey Berger. She's written several books too, and a good place to start is *Simple habits for complex times*. Jennifer Garvey Berger and Keith Johnston (Stanford University Press, 2015).

A great guide to developing yourself based on adult development research comes from *Upgrade, building your capacity for complexity*. Karen Ellis and Robert Boston (Leaderspace, 2019).

And if you're interested in how these ideas apply on an organisational level, see *Reinventing organisations*. Frederic Laloux (Nelson Parker, 2014).

[1] For more on constructive-developmental theory, see Cook-Greuter, S. (2004) and Torbert, W. R. (2004).

[2] Rooke, D., Fisher, D., Torbert, W. R. (2003).

[3] Kegan, R. (1995).

[4] The principle of letting go, and acquiring new work values comes from Charam, R., Drotter, S., & Noel. J. (2011).

[5] Kegan, R., Lahey, L., Fleming, A. and Miller, M. (2014).

Chapter 3. Self-awareness as the key to change

In the last two chapters I've explained some of the key foundations that shape who we are – our personality, our responses to our environment, and the available worldviews from which we make sense of the world. You might be wondering what all this has to do with healthy high performance, and the answer is that these foundations enable us to understand how we can change and grow. Pure behaviourists who train rats and pigeons in labs might disagree of course, but as adult human beings I believe that self-awareness is central to change. I will explain why and how in this chapter.

Summary

- If you want to change, you must first become aware of your motivational strategies and world views.
- This is self-awareness.
- Self-awareness is not always easy and requires practice.
- Inner experience comprises thoughts, emotions, and patterns.
- Motivational strategies are important patterns, that can enable or block growth in a process called 'immunity to change'.
- Change comes from awareness, acceptance, experiments and forming new habits.
- The right 1% change is enough to make a big difference.

Self-awareness is the key to change. Without it, we are doomed to keep repeating habitual patterns of thinking and behaviour. With self-awareness comes the possibility of interrupting a habit and making a fresh choice.[1] I define self-awareness as the capacity to reflect on thoughts, feelings, assumptions, and patterns of behaviour with a degree of objectivity. It is the ability to 'have' a thought or feeling rather than being 'had' by it. People vary in their level of self-awareness and this capacity develops over time and with practice. When people first become curious about their inner world the experience can be a little daunting. I liken it to an exercise novice going to the gym for the first time. The gym is full of intimidating people and strange equipment and feels strange and confusing. With a bit of instruction and commitment, the process of weight training becomes familiar, and even enjoyable. Likewise, exploring your inner world of thoughts and feelings gets easier with practice.

Different cultures have different expectations and language for inner experience too, adding to the wide range of individual differences in the capacity to self-reflect:

> **How are you?**
> Many years ago, when my children were very young, an au pair lived with our family for six months. Maria was from Slovakia and this was her first experience living in a foreign country. Her English was improving, but she still wasn't totally fluent. One evening I came into the kitchen to find her sitting at the table. "Jon, the English are very strange". I sat down with a cup of tea and listened. "Today someone said to me 'How are you?', but they didn't really care about what I said next." She seemed puzzled, and even troubled as she spoke. I explained that 'How are you?' is often used as a polite greeting. "Yes" she replied, "but back home only a good friend asks, 'how are you?' and then they would expect to talk about this for at least twenty minutes!"

Often the answer to "How are you?" is 'fine' or "ok" – bland comments that keep the social interaction going but revealing little real insight. And this is fine in many situations – as Maria discovered, a deep and reflective conversation is often NOT expected in a casual conversation in Britain! But this also means that you may have learned to stay at a superficial level that makes it harder to develop greater self-awareness. In order to help develop self-awareness let's understand the different ingredients of inner experience and how they connect. This is a map and like all maps, it is only an approximation of reality. It might however be useful, to help you get better at noticing what's happening inside your head and heart.

Map of inner experience

Thoughts are the basic building block of inner experience and make up the incessant inner dialogue we all experience. At their simplest level, thoughts are descriptions of what we are noticing at the time, memories of the past, or concerns about the future.

Judgements or opinions are thoughts that categorise what you are experiencing; as good or bad, new or old, beautiful or ugly. They are subjective, which means that different people may judge the same event in different ways.

Assumptions are the stories you tell to explain the world. They are a useful form of shorthand that simplify and speed up your responses to external events and threats. Your ancestors were the ones who survived because they formed the most useful assumptions about the dangers of large animals!

Emotions or feelings are physical sensations that add an extra level of information about a situation and motivate you to action. Emotions will either move you toward something you judge is good, or away from situations you judge are dangerous. "Toward" emotions include feeling happy, excited, and loving while "away" emotions include feeling angry, sad, or bored. Emotions are objective because they are real experiences, although some are based on subjective judgements. Another person may have a different emotional response to a situation than you do, but that does not make either of you right or wrong.

Patterns are repeating forms of thinking and emotion that connect to behaviour. The various motivational strategies we introduced in the first two chapters are a specific type of pattern. They exist at a level of abstraction that can be hard to spot without careful attention and they also take a certain amount of life experience to register.

Here are some examples:

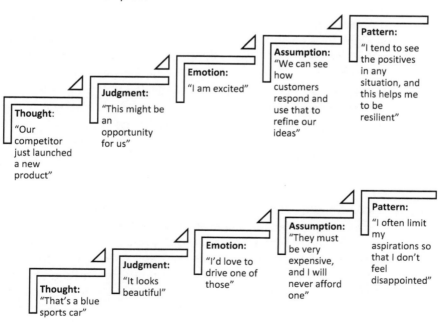

Even with these simple examples, you will realise that different people will have very different thoughts, judgements, assumptions, and patterns in the same situation. Many people probably wouldn't even notice the sports car in the first place! We will each interpret and experience the world based on our personality, worldview and the motivational strategies we have developed through our lives.

AN EXERCISE TO DEVELOP SELF-AWARENESS

I often use an exercise from *Gestalt Therapy* called 'see, imagine, feel' to help people explore their inner world and start to clarify the difference between thoughts, judgements, assumptions and feelings. The exercise involves naming out loud something you can see (or hear) about another person. "I see you have your arms crossed", or "I hear you speaking softly". This is intended to be an objective description, but it is surprisingly hard to do. Rather than a description, many go

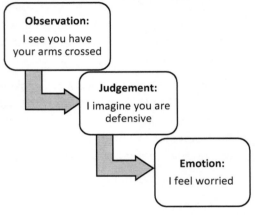

Observation:
I see you have your arms crossed

Judgement:
I imagine you are defensive

Emotion:
I feel worried

straight to their interpretation: "I see you are feeling defensive today", or "You don't sound confident". You do not actually 'see' defensiveness or 'hear' a lack of confidence, instead you assume these are true based on the available evidence. It may be true that the other person IS feeling defensive or lacking confidence, or they may simply be more comfortable with crossed arms or have a sore throat. The exercise invites you to slow down and make your assumptions explicit: "I see you have your arms crossed and I *imagine* you are defensive", "I hear your voice is soft and I *imagine* you are not feeling confident". This is challenging and at times uncomfortable because these observations and interpretations normally stay safely tucked away between your ears. Although not necessarily obvious to the other person, your judgements influence your emotions, and hence your behaviour. The final part of the exercise is even tougher – to shift attention inwards and notice how you feel, and then make this explicit too: "I see you have your arms crossed, I imagine you are defensive, and I feel worried." "I hear your voice is hesitant, I imagine you are not feeling confident, and I feel supportive". It can be hard to find the right word for an emotion – sometimes no particular emotion is evoked, sometimes it is a mixture, and sometimes you just do not know. (There is also a rare psychological condition called alexithymia, in which people are unable to distinguish their emotional and physical feelings).[2]

Here is a real example from one of my coaching clients:

Alan was a senior finance professional in a major enterprise. He knew from his boss's feedback that he was not making a positive impact and was failing to contribute confidently to Board meetings. This was particularly frustrating because Alan's expertise and financial insights were widely recognised and respected. I began with a three-way meeting with Alan and his boss, who provided frank and constructive feedback. Even more importantly, this interaction provided me with a valuable insight into Alan's relationship with his boss. I noticed that Alan's demeanour changed the moment his boss walked into the room, his voice softened, he said little, and he looked down. Exploring this behaviour further in the coaching sessions led Alan to realise that meeting his boss, or anyone more senior to him, triggered an unhelpful response that was limiting his effectiveness. His early life experience had led Alan to believe that he had to be perfect in the eyes of his parents to gain their approval. Whilst this belief had a positive impact on his drive and ambition, it also limited his confidence and meant that unless he was 100% sure of himself, he would say nothing because he was fearful of being wrong. This profound insight unlocked Alan's confidence and he started to experiment with the 80/20 principle; speaking up when he felt at least 80% sure of his view and seeking solutions that were 'good enough' rather than perfect. This simple change led to a remarkable increase in self-awareness and self-confidence, which in turn created a virtuous circle, as his team and boss noticed the positive difference in Alan's impact. I learned later that he was promoted less than a year after this intervention.

Self-awareness takes practice, it is not always easy or obvious, and often when you try to reflect, you find a jumbled mix of thoughts, feelings and physical sensations. The first stage of improving self-awareness – and increasing your capacity to grow, learn and perform – is to understand how you are adding to reality through your judgements and assumptions. Then to understand how these thoughts *about* reality shape your experience, feelings and actions. By calling out and noticing your own thoughts, assumptions and emotions you create a finer appreciation for your current reality and open the space for a different and potentially more constructive series of thoughts, feelings and actions.

With practice and attention, you will also start to notice the underlying patterns of how you respond in different situations, particularly when you feel threatened. Many of the most significant patterns will be the motivational strategies you developed early in life to meet your basic psychological needs. We discussed some of the typical motivational patterns in Chapter 1, when we are strongly driven by the need for security, acceptance and control. Knowing when these needs are in play is a vital step in achieving a mature level of self-awareness, because it opens the possibility for profound learning.

Immunity to change

There are two immediate challenges in working with underlying motivational strategies. The first is to identify them. By their nature they are deeply ingrained, have been at least somewhat effective, and lie embedded in the worldview from which we operate. They often sit in our blind spots – which means we do not see our own patterns, but others do! The second challenge is, what do we do with them once they have been identified? How do we change them?

Fortunately, Harvard psychologists Robert Kegan and Lisa Lahey have developed a powerful process that can help with both these challenges.[3] Their approach is based on asking a series of carefully framed questions that surface the underlying, and usually unacknowledged, tension between what we aspire to do and a hidden motivational pattern that we believe is keeping us safe. They call this underlying belief a 'competing commitment' that creates an immunity to change. A competing commitment often explains why our attempts to change fail.

Let's bring this to life through an example.

James (remember we met him in Chapter 1), our hardworking property developer, wants to empower Steve, a senior member of his team, to take the lead on some client relationships. This makes good sense, because it will spread the workload and enable his firm to take on more projects by breaking the bottleneck caused by his personal involvement at every stage of the deal. Yet he finds it difficult to step back and, even worse, often jumps into a deal once its underway. This creates frustration for Steve and confusion for clients.

Here's how an immunity to change conversation might go with James:

So, James, what new behaviour are you committed to?

I want to get out of the way and let Steve develop his own client relationships. I know I slow things down too much if I have to be involved at every step, so I want to delegate more to him.

Can you describe what you are doing, or not doing, that's preventing you from fully delegating to Steve?

Well, I notice that I still come along to client meetings even when I have asked Steve to take the lead.

Imagine you did not go to the client meetings in person, what might you worry about?

I don't feel comfortable without knowing all the detail of the deal myself. I'd worry that Steve might miss something important. I am afraid of the deal going wrong if I don't have sight of everything.

So, by going along to the client meeting, what are you are trying to avoid, or stop from happening? Can we frame this as a commitment towards something, even if that feels a bit wrong?

I might also be committed to holding onto the details even if it means disempowering Steve.

What do you assume it would mean if you let go of the detail?

I assume that if I don't have an eye on the detail, things will go wrong, and that will cost me money and reputation, which would mean I have lost control of my business. And I'd feel like I have failed if that happened.

The Immunity to Change questions help James to discover a competing commitment that is sabotaging his stated desire to delegate more. While he wants to delegate more, he is also committed to not losing control. The fact that he is not delegating simply shows that the competing commitment (to *not* losing control) is more powerful than his aspiration (to delegate more). This is proved because his actual behaviour – always turning up at the meetings – is logically consistent with the competing commitment. Underlying James' competing commitment is what Kegan and Lahey call a 'Big Assumption'. In this case, James assumes that losing control will lead to all sorts of serious difficulties that would threaten to his business, and more importantly his self-esteem. There is a real strength of feeling accompanying this belief that fuels his reluctance to delegate more, even though he "knows" delegating is the right thing to do.

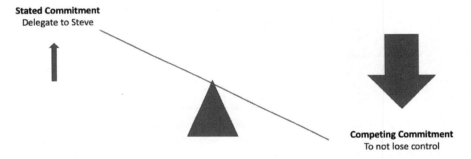

Stated Commitment
Delegate to Steve

Competing Commitment
To not lose control

Figure 1 Steve's competing commitment

I have worked through the immunity to change process with hundreds of people over the years, and it almost always leads to an unsettling revelation that we are held back by fears about being alone, powerless, a failure, out of control, unloved or rejected, stupid, or wrong. These fears feel *fundamental* because they all relate to the ego's survival needs for security, control and acceptance, which in turn drive our motivational strategies. If you have any doubt about your own motivational strategies, the immunity to change process provides a powerful insight that increases self-awareness. Regardless of anything else this is very useful because it allows us to move the Big Assumption from 'behind our eyes', to something 'in front of our eyes' that we can consider more objectively. Making the Big Assumption explicit and holding it up to the light of day, we realise that in many circumstances the fear is unjustified. It may even sound a bit silly if we say it out loud: "I assume that if I get into a disagreement, I will lose my job", "I assume that if I do not produce perfect work people will think I am a failure", "I assume if I do not keep control of everything my business and I will fail". We can recognise instead that while giving up control may not feel comfortable, it is not life-threatening either. The fear behind our Big Assumptions can lock us into a particular worldview, serving as a brake on our natural growth. Or it can act like a psychic wormhole that takes us back to an earlier worldview when triggered by a stressful situation. Kegan calls this this the 'one big thing' that needs attention at a given time in life.

Enabling change

Let's return to James, who by this time is feeling usefully unsettled. How does he use his newfound awareness to make the changes he seeks in his leadership? A range of tools and tactics are available, and here is how they help James move forward with his desired change.

WRITE A BIOGRAPHY OF YOUR BIG ASSUMPTION

Your motivational patterns started early, as part of your ego's survival strategy to stay safe, in control or in contact with others. Explore for yourself when and how these might have started. Think back to your own early family and school experiences – were there any significant events or challenges? What sort of behaviour did your parents or caregivers praise or criticise? What was acceptable and what wasn't? What sort of things 'rocked the boat'? How was conflict managed? Can you remember how you felt when things were good, and when they were not so good? Some people find it helpful to sit and write the old-fashioned way with a pen and paper. If you do find the origins (and some people do not), remind yourself that this was your best attempt to survive and stay safe in the past, and it does not have to be your response now. A useful affirmation is 'that was then, this is now.'

> James reflects on his own history and recalls his life as a young boy, often feeling scared and uncertain. He comes to see how his drive and commitment are an adaptive response to this early experience that has helped him to build a successful business. He has come to equate having money with having the control and safety he lacked when young.

SELF-AWARENESS

Notice *where* the big assumption shows up in your life. It is likely you will start to realise that it crops up in different situations, both at work and at home. The process of noticing builds mental space between you and the assumption, so that it starts to become a thing you can look at, rather than a frame you look through. Stay alert to counterexamples where the assumption *does not* hold, or the effects *are not* as severe as you imagine. These examples are important evidence that can free up your behaviour.

James becomes curious about his assumption, and to his surprise notices that the more confidence he has in other people, the more willing he is to let go of direct control.

TEST THE BIG ASSUMPTION

Become a scientist and consider your assumption as a working hypothesis rather than the truth. Carefully, push your boundaries and experiment with behaviour that is counter to how a big assumption would have you act. Experiments will also help you discover the specific situations, including triggers, that provoke your big assumption into action. You can seek feedback from a trusted colleague to help you gauge the impact of your experiments, and gradually increase the scale of the experiment. For example, many years ago when I was working on my Big Assumption that "if I disagree with someone, they will reject me", I chose to use the opportunity of attending a leadership programme to experiment with speaking with more candour. I committed to always speaking up even if I thought my views might be controversial or (as I feared) unwelcome. At the end of the week my fellow participants shared their feedback, and I was pleased and relieved to hear that they had welcomed my forthright contributions.

James makes a list of the various situations in which he could delegate and let Steve take the lead. He recognises that there are some critical times where it is essential that he stays involved, particularly when he has a long-standing relationship with the client, and they trust him personally. There are other routine meetings where this isn't so important, and there is a much lower risk of things going wrong if he isn't present. He decides to start by delegating the routine meetings to Steve.

DEAL WITH EMOTIONAL TRIGGERS

As you pay attention to your behaviour and start to experiment, you may notice that specific situations provoke a powerful negative emotional response. These triggers flare when your security needs are unexpectedly or strongly challenged. It is important to learn to spot these situations early to give yourself the best chance of managing your emotional response in the moment. You may find that when triggered, your inner critic starts to harangue you and nag "you idiot, you're hopeless, you're doing that again" or perhaps your inner coach gives a pep talk "never mind, stay positive, you can do it!" While you might think that the goal is to silence the critic and listen to the coach, a more productive approach is to do neither. Paradoxically, simply noticing and accepting your inner reality, rather than fighting or cajoling, is the key to change. This insight draws on the ancient practice of mindfulness, as well as contemporary neuroscience. When you develop the capacity to notice your thoughts and feelings you shift your brain activity from the amygdala (centre of emotional processing) to the frontal cortex (centre of your executive function). Once the frontal cortex is re-engaged, you can make a choice. Formally choosing what you want is a powerful step, that orients your energy and attention towards constructive action. We will come back to this in Chapter 6.

Here's a simple process that you can practise when you are emotionally triggered:

1. **Notice** – be aware of your thinking, behaviour and feelings without judging yourself
2. **Name** – the emotions you are feeling
3. **Be Present** – bring your attention into the here and now. Breathe.
4. **Choose** – what do you want to do next? How can you respond rather than react right now?

> *The people in James' company quickly learn that if there is one thing that James hates, it is unexpected bad news. Being caught out is a powerful trigger that evokes a strong and unhelpful emotional response in James – anger, a raised voice and table thumping. By recognising this trigger and applying the simple process of noticing, naming, being present and choosing, James starts to catch himself and respond to unexpected events a little more calmly.*

DEVELOP NEW HABITS
The process I have just described works because it helps you to inhibit your brain's habitual, automatic response. The brain's capacity to create habits is both a gift because it allows you to do difficult things quickly and efficiently without using up limited energy and attention, and a challenge because it can be hard to change an established but unhelpful habit. Recent

developments in the science of habits[4] have led to simple, yet effective approaches to behaviour change.

The first step is to be very clear about your desired new behaviour and the specific situations in which you want it to apply. It is important to start small, with a 'stepping stone' change that you are almost certain you can achieve, and which will move you closer to your ultimate goal. This is the choice you will make, either when emotionally triggered or when the triggering event is more mundane. You also need to be very clear about why this new behaviour is important to you, and the benefits it will bring. It takes anything from 20 – 40 days to really embed a new habit, and it helps if you have regular feedback and someone to provide accountability.

Here is an example of the habit change formula that James employs to help change how he works with Steve:

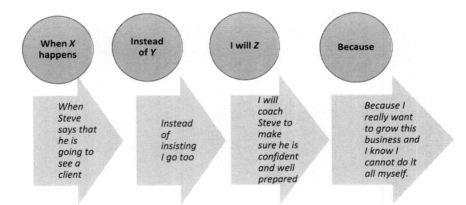

As a result of all this work, James improves his ability to delegate to Steve, whose confidence grows too. This frees up James' time to develop new client relationships and he achieves his goals of faster work throughput and better team morale.

The power of 1%

I often draw on high performance sport to illustrate the big impact that a small change can make. For an elite competitor, 4th place is often a painful result because it proves that you are world-class, but there is no medal to show for it. Yet as the following table shows, even a 1% difference can be enough to get onto the podium.[5] Here are results of a range of 4th place finishers from the Rio 2016 Olympics and Paralympics. What if they had been 1% faster?

Rio 2016 Event	4ᵗʰ place	1% better?	Result
Athletics Men's 100m	9.93	9.83	Silver
Swimming Men's 100m	47.88	47.40	Gold
Canoe Slalom Men's K1	89.02	88.13	Gold
Cycling Women's road race	3:51.27	3.49.48	Gold
Rowing Women's Eight	6.05.48	6.01.82	Silver
Para Triathlon Men PT2	1.12.51	1.11.17	Gold

Figure 2 Comparison of 1st to 4th place, 2016 Olympic and Paralympic Games

Clearly, it is not as simple as just trying 1% harder! Successful performance in sport requires the careful coordination and delivery of physical, technical, psychological and logistical factors at exactly the right time. Likewise, trying harder is unlikely to be the difference that makes a difference for you. In each of the three following chapters, I suggest simple, practical new habits that will help you think, relate and act more effectively. Consider each of these as potential 1% changes in your own performance.

Conclusion

I have worked with many people like James and seen their relief when they realise that they can grow and change. Often talented, bright people are held back from change because they have learned to conflate their talent and intelligence with their self-worth. This makes it hard to experiment because there is a lot on the line emotionally. They are fearful of letting go of the things that have helped them in the past, yet by considering new possibilities with an open mindset, a degree of humility, and a touch of courage, positive change becomes possible.

Want to know more?

For a thorough guide that will help you apply the competing commitments framework individually and with teams, see *Immunity to Change, how to overcome it and unlock the potential of yourself and your organization* by

Robert Kegan and Lisa Laskow Lahey (Harvard Business School Publishing, 2009).

There are now many resources available on using habits to support change, however James Clear is preeminent, and his website is worth a look. See his book *Atomic Habits, an easy and proven way to build good habits and break bad ones.* (Random House Press, 2018).

---

[1] This is based on the principles of emotional intelligence. See Goleman, D. (2005).

[2] For discussion of Alexithymia see Autistica at https://www.autistica.org.uk/what-is-autism/anxiety-and-autism-hub/alexithymia

[3] Kegan, R. & Lahey, L.L. (2009).

[4] For example, see Clear, J. (2018).

[5] Olympics results available at https://olympics.com/en/olympic-games/rio-2016, Paralympic result available at https://www.paralympic.org/rio-2016/results

Section 2. The ART of Performance

Now that we've laid the Foundations, we're ready to get into the individual behaviours that you can use to create healthy, sustained high performance. This section offers three chapters devoted to how you think, relate and act, showing what you can do to get better at each of these capacities. I suggest specific new habits that will help you sustain consistent change.

Chapter 4. Think straight

We are going to start our exploration of the ART of healthy high performance with thinking. I will explain what goes wrong with our thinking when we are stressed or threatened – we become more prone to a range of distortions and mental biases that limit creativity and can lead to bad decisions. I will show you practical approaches to better thinking alone and with others.

Summary

- We often experience working life as threatening.
- Threat leads to defensive thinking – a narrow focus, low creativity and a tendency to blame and justify.
- A range of inbuilt biases also interfere with quality thinking.
- Increasing self-awareness helps counter defensive thinking, biases and assumptions.
- Shifting perspective is essential.
- Thinking with others is a separate skill that needs to be developed.

Why thinking matters

The capacity to think is central to being human; the name of our species Homo sapiens means "wise and discerning person". The activity between our ears shapes how we relate, what we feel and what we do. This influence is not a one-way flow, and our relationships, emotions and actions influence our thinking in a complex web of interactions we call consciousness. Thinking that is disconnected from action and relationships means that your head is in the clouds, lost in theory. Yet trying to perform without engaging your intellect leaves you stuck in a rut, a loyal foot soldier mindlessly following habitual behaviour.

Effective thinking is not simply a matter of intelligence, just as having a powerful engine is insufficient for a well-designed car. Notions of a single, all-encompassing IQ measure have been overtaken by an understanding that there are many different types of intelligence, that are significantly shaped by culture and context.[1] What it means to be smart depends on where you live, because different environments create different adaptive demands. A more important factor than IQ is learning HOW to think, and this capacity can grow and evolve over time. In this chapter I want to start by laying out three different ways in which the quality of thinking is compromised; by psychologically unsafe work environments, through our ingrained cognitive biases, and by our use of assumptions to short cut novel thinking. I will then provide practical guidelines that can help mitigate these problems and improve the quality of your thinking.

How working life distorts thinking – and how our thinking distorts working life

A basic premise of this book is that much of modern working life creates conditions which we perceive as threatening. Under these conditions, our brains respond in ways that have proved to be useful for our survival in the past. Unfortunately, many of these patterns are counter-productive in our post-modern world. As we learn more about the functioning of the mind, we can increase our capacity to spot these thinking patterns, counteract them, and establish the conditions for healthier and more productive thinking.

What happens inside our heads when we feel vulnerable? It depends on the nature and severity of the perceived threat, and whether we believe it is an acute, immediate threat (we are wired to respond fast to these) or a longer term, chronic danger (we are generally poor at responding to these). Unless you are serving in the military, the police, prison or emergency services, few people face acute physical danger at work. Threats in the modern working world are more likely to be perceived dangers to our psychological well-being, which David Rock[2] has usefully summarised using the acronym SCARF:

Status	is my importance relative to others being challenged?
Certainty	how unsure do I feel about what's going to happen in the future?
Autonomy	do I feel like I am losing, or have lost, control over things that matter to me?
Relatedness	is there a risk of conflict?
Fairness	do I feel that I am being treated unfairly?

Sadly, most working environments regularly create conditions where we feel that our status, certainty, or autonomy are threatened, let alone bring us into conflict or situations that feel unfair. For example, being criticized by your boss in public might feel both unfair and a challenge to your status. Not being able to get an answer from a client when you are trying to meet a sales target creates uncertainty. A new team member with a radically different working style might trigger a fear about relatedness. And so on, and so on. You can probably think of your own examples.

When we feel threatened, the mind responds by defensive thinking, which means that you:

- **Narrow your focus and stop taking on new information**
  Tunnel vision might help in a life and death situation when you need to preserve your resources by ignoring anything outside your immediate field of view. But it can also mean that you miss important and relevant facts that could shift the meaning of a problem or lead to new solutions.

- **Lose your capacity to think creatively and flexibly**
  Narrowing attention also leads to 'functional fixedness'. When this occurs, you take an inflexible view of resources and people that limits creative possibilities. You miss the possibility of asking your office receptionist to bring a fresh perspective in a marketing meeting, because you have become stuck in your view of her as 'only' the receptionist.

- **Defend and justify your own position**
  Losing status feels painful, so we fight hard to maintain it by doubling down on our own positions. Whilst it is just as counter-productive to 'roll over' when your idea is challenged, there is a difference between engaging in a constructive exploration to find the best solution and 'dying in a ditch' to defend your point of view.

- **Blame others for your situation**
  Another way to avoid the pain of being wrong, or appearing weak, is to avoid taking personal responsibility and to deflect the blame onto others. While external factors and other people's behaviour may well contribute to a challenging situation, defensive thinking leads to seeking the cause by looking out the window far more than looking in the mirror.

Defensive thinking is contagious. I saw this in one client organisation where a team leader was stuck in defensive thinking.

Tony led a team of engineers in an overworked, under-funded local authority. He had worked there for nearly thirty years and had seen new administrations come and go, each time being promised more resources and each time being disappointed. He had become deeply cynical and defensive. This created a toxic, unproductive climate where no-one was willing to suggest new ideas or speak out unless it was to complain and gossip. These behaviours confirmed a belief that the conditions were not safe and fed a cycle of silence (staying quiet and keeping your head down) or violence (criticizing and sniping). As a result, the quality of thinking was severely limited, and his department lacked creativity and innovation. ('Silence and violence' are also signs of a lack of psychological safety, this will be discussed in Chapter 7.)

A different type of defensive thinking can occur in the face of long-term threats and challenges. When the impact of a problem is far in the future, and we do not feel immediate pain, we often respond by simply ignoring it. Margaret Heffernan describes this as wilful blindness,[3] and it is another form of self-protection. It is particularly relevant when acting now would require me to change or challenge my current beliefs. This is one reason why acting on climate change has been a hard sell, at least while the impact is perceived to be far away in time or space.

Cognitive biases – inbuilt thinking problems

Even in relatively safe environments, the human mind has many quirks that can interfere with clear thinking. Cognitive biases occur independently of intelligence; in fact researchers have found that highly intelligent people are more prone to 'dysrationalia' – irrational decision making. This can be due to 'earned dogmatism' – a belief that because I have acquired a high level of expertise in one field, I must be equally clever in all fields. This explains why scammers are often most successful with highly intelligent people who know nothing about financial affairs.[4] Another reason is that having higher processing power can lead people to rely on fast intuitive thinking, rather than taking the time to think more carefully about an issue. Effective performers have learned what situations are best served by intuitive responses, and which benefit from a planned approach to decision making. Sport provides a powerful example of when this goes right – and wrong. For a golfer standing over a simple one metre putt, it is not the time to go into a detailed breakdown of the putting stroke, and to do so invites 'paralysis by analysis' and poor execution. However, the same golfer, when faced with a long and tricky approach to a green may benefit from pausing and thinking through different options, weighing up the risks and benefits of attacking the hole or playing it safe and laying up.

One of the most common problems I see in the work environment is due to confirmatory bias – the tendency to ignore facts that challenge a choice you have already made, and only pay attention to facts that back up your decision.[5] One client, a Managing Director, experienced this after appointing a new Finance Director. He had invested considerable time and effort in the recruitment process and felt convinced he had made the right choice. Initially the new appointment looked successful, but noises started to emerge from the Finance department about unprofessional behaviour, and even worse, bullying. At the same time the Managing Director was pleased with the new reporting systems and cost savings that the Finance Director was initiating that were making an immediate impact on the bottom line. It took more time than it should for him to take seriously the mounting criticism of the Finance Director's behaviour, allowing morale in the Finance team to plummet and losing several valued team members, because he insisted on only listening to the evidence that backed his original decision. Confirmatory bias is a form of cognitive dissonance; once I take a public stance my identity and self-esteem start to become enmeshed. So even if the facts say otherwise, cognitive dissonance means I will find it impossible to admit I am wrong. I will become more and more stubborn in my beliefs because to change my mind will feel like a mortal blow to my identity, values and reputation – unless I develop the humility to look for and acknowledge the flaws in my own thinking.

Another powerful bias shows up when people are required to think together. The drive to conform has long been recognised as a problem for clear thinking. Termed 'groupthink',[6] it was first identified after an analysis of President Kennedy's disastrous decision to support an invasion of Cuba in 1962. Despite serious reservations about the plan, none of Kennedy's advisors were willing to be the first to speak out and challenge the apparent consensus, or to be seen to be disloyal to the charismatic and popular President. Healthy conflict and an acceptance of challenge are essential to avoid this trap.

The perils of short cuts – how assumptions can get in the way

Henry Ford was reported to have said "thinking is the hardest work there is, which is why so little of it gets done". Thinking is indeed hard work, and the brain is highly energy intensive, which is why we have evolved to take cognitive short cuts that make it easier. These short cuts are assumptions, like computer algorithms, which are predetermined rules for interpreting, understanding, and responding to situations. Clearly, many assumptions are helpful and even essential for daily life. I have an assumption that a red traffic light means I stop my car. I have an assumption that someone extending their hand to me in a meeting means I should extend mine too and shake hands. I have an assumption that if I do not know something, I can use Google to find an answer. Yet assumptions can also become outdated, limiting or just plain wrong. Here is a story I spotted many years ago in a daily newspaper:[7]

Commuter suffers signal failure on 8am to Waterloo
A senior administrator was tracked by an undercover detective and accused of stalking because he kept looking at a female fellow passenger he thought was attracted to him, a court heard yesterday. Mr P and Mrs M had seen each other regularly on the 8am train to work, the court heard. But they both completely misread the signals. She initially looked at him because she was distracted by his fiddling behind his newspaper. He wrongly believed she was attracted to him. As he attempted to reciprocate what he imagined were her attempts to make eye contact with him, the combination of his smiles and continual fidgeting led her to imagine that something more sinister was going on. But Mrs M conceded under questioning that she could not see whether Mr P was doing anything behind his newspaper and had only thought that he might be "doing disgusting things". He, meanwhile, said it was all his fault. He believed she was attracted to him and the more she looked at him, the more he tried to reciprocate. "I do not deny looking at the dear lady," he said. "I thought she was looking at me. I totally misread the position and I extend my sincere apologies to her. It is my fault for picking up the wrong vibes."
Dismissing the case, the Magistrate said Mrs M's admission that she had no idea what Mr P was doing behind his newspaper was a "whole world away from the allegations that resulted in his arrest." He added "There is no doubt at all that both parties misread the situation. I am quite satisfied that no jury could convict on this evidence and the charge is dismissed."

On a corporate level, faulty assumptions can lead to far worse than embarrassment. A powerful example comes from Kodak, a company that at its peak was worth $31B, with $16B annual revenues in 1996. Its core business was selling and processing film, and despite inventing the first digital camera in 1975, its leaders were limited by several faulty assumptions. The company invested billions to develop high quality professional cameras, assuming the new digital technology would be of no interest to consumers. They acquired Ofoto, an early online photo sharing website in 2001, but assumed that people would still want to print their photos and so they tried to use Ofoto to drive income to their traditional printing business. Kodak filed for bankruptcy in 2011 and survives today as a niche player in specialist industrial cameras.[8]

How to improve the quality of your thinking

Given all these challenges, you might start to despair that you will ever think clearly again! Fortunately, there are simple, pragmatic ways to get better at thinking and decision making. Taken together these will help you think more systemically – consider more perspectives - and avoid the pitfalls we have just discussed. We are going to look at three approaches: increasing self-awareness, challenging assumptions, and increasing the number of perspectives you take on an issue.

SELF-AWARENESS
Developing awareness of *how* you think, known as meta-awareness, is a powerful first step to improving the quality of your thinking. This means that your thinking is no longer something that just happens. Instead, you can reflect on it and notice the patterns of thoughts and feelings that drive your behaviour. This in turns allows you to challenge and start to change your habitual ways of thinking, reducing the effects of biases and assumptions.

A simple tool to develop your self-awareness is to check whether you are "above or below the line." [9] Being below the line means that you are engaging in defensive thinking – the default, automatic response to threatening situations that we discussed earlier. In this state of mind, I become defensive and closed, blame others, and make excuses for my own behaviour (or lack of it).

Being above the line means making a conscious choice to take a constructive attitude and frame the situation as a challenge rather than a threat. When I am above the line, I can perceive a difficult situation as an opportunity to learn. I will be curious and open to different points of view. I will take ownership for my contributions and behaviour (whether it has been helpful or not). My language will be about the action I can take to implement a solution or do something constructive.

We all fluctuate between being above and below the line, and while it is normal to go below the line on occasion, it is not a good place to spend a lot of time! Certain situations or relationships may be particularly strong triggers to going below the line, so it is important to stay aware and ask; "where am I now?" Being aware of whether I am below the line and thinking defensively in any given moment is an essential first step in making a change to a more constructive mindset.

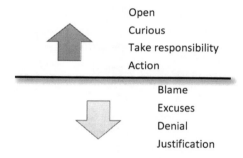

Open
Curious
Take responsibility
Action

Blame
Excuses
Denial
Justification

Figure 3 Where are you? Above or below the line.

CHALLENGE YOUR ASSUMPTIONS - "HOW MIGHT I BE WRONG?"

Being above the line is shorthand for a constructive, curious and questioning mindset in which you are open to learning. One of the most important questions that you can ask from above the line is "how might I be wrong?" This may seem a strange question to ask, because it might imply a lack of confidence quite at odds with normal convention. Yet it is a powerful question because it opens up space from the most dangerous assumption of all – the fervent belief that I am right, and therefore others are wrong. This assumption makes it all too easy to polarise around a contentious issue and see the 'other side' as the villains who are totally and always wrong. And if they are the villains, I must be the hero, and the more this identity becomes central to me the more attached I become to my beliefs and ideas. But we do not live in a black and white world, and if I can look without fear for my own identity, I will start to recognise that any position has some merit, no matter how minor.[10]

This requires humility, a quality I discovered is important in many, at times surprising, domains:

Many years ago, when I was working as a sport psychologist with the British Olympic team, I was attending an official team function before the start of competition. I struck up conversation with a senior naval officer, and as we discussed the challenges of Olympic performance, I suggested that the pressure in sport must be nothing compared to that experienced in combat. He smiled, and said "come with me, there are a couple of chaps here you should meet." We walked over to the fringe of the crowd, where three tall, well-built men in casual shirts and chinos were standing quietly. My naval friend made a brief introduction and left. I explained my role, curious about who they were. Speaking quietly, they explained they were members of the SAS, Britain's elite commando force, who just happened to be in town at the same time as the Olympics "enjoying the sun." Their answer to my question about the key to clear thinking and performance under pressure? "It is all to do with humility". Not the answer I was expecting at all! They went on to explain that survival and success in their dangerous, high stakes environment came not from being tough and knowing it all, but from having the humility to take feedback and learn, fast. Any aspiring SAS member without the humility to learn did not last long, because they were seen as a danger to themselves and their squad mates.

Having the humility to consider that you might be wrong is a wonderful antidote to tunnel vision and functional fixedness, as it takes your thinking into new territory and invites you to challenge other assumptions. One of my favourite approaches is to go on a sacred cow hunt, described in the book *Sacred Cows make the best burgers*.[11] A sacred cow is:

"an outmoded belief, assumption, practice, policy, system, or strategy, generally invisible, that inhibits change and prevents responsiveness to new opportunities."

Here are questions I have adapted from his book that will help you spot your sacred cows:

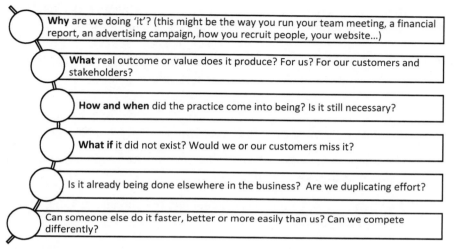

Why are we doing 'it'? (this might be the way you run your team meeting, a financial report, an advertising campaign, how you recruit people, your website...)

What real outcome or value does it produce? For us? For our customers and stakeholders?

How and when did the practice come into being? Is it still necessary?

What if it did not exist? Would we or our customers miss it?

Is it already being done elsewhere in the business? Are we duplicating effort?

Can someone else do it faster, better or more easily than us? Can we compete differently?

I introduced these questions to a commercial property team, who realised with horror that their company had been producing a market report for their clients for more than thirty years without ever refreshing the format. A pharmaceutical company I worked with was prompted to totally change how they engaged with the government regulator, which led to a real breakthrough in their ability to navigate a tortuous funding approval process.

You can also challenge functional fixedness and rigid thinking by using 'what if' questions.[12] What if questions work by breaking you out of your current thinking patterns into novel territory. The first answers you get may not seem practical, but they can serve as useful stepping-stones to a practical solution. For example, you could vary the time frame of your problem; what if it had to be solved in 1 hour? What if we had 10 years? You might vary the resources available; what if we had an unlimited budget? What if we only had £500?

SHIFT PERSPECTIVE

Going below the line leads to becoming stuck in a self-centred orientation, in which you blame and dehumanise others. To counter this, another powerful thinking strategy is to deliberately shift perspective and de-centre from your own point of view. There are several ways of doing this. The simplest is to literally shift perspective by getting up and moving, going for a walk, and changing your environment. You can also think about a problem from the views of the different stakeholders. This may sound obvious, but how often have you felt frustrated when a business changes its operations to make life easier for itself and harder for you as a customer?

Another good option where there is conflict or impasse is the 'perceptual positions'[13] technique in which you work through:

1st Position: My own point of view - *I*

2nd Position: The other person or party's point of view - *you*

3rd Position: The view of an independent observer watching *the interaction between 1 and 2*.

4th Position: A high altitude view, observing how positions 1, 2 and 3 fit within a bigger system – *it*

This process requires some imagination and empathy. 1st position is the natural starting point for most people, and where you stay if you are below the line. You may discover from taking the 2nd position that you simply do not know how someone else is feeling, or what their priorities are, in which case a useful step is to go and find out. Taking the 3rd position can reveal useful insights about the pattern of communication and the relationship between you. And stepping back to the 4th position puts a problem into a bigger context, helping you appreciate the myriad of factors that are at play. It is like changing your altitude when looking at Google maps. By zooming up you change the scale, losing granular detail but seeing the bigger context. In addition to considering these static positions, you can add a powerful dimension by considering the effect of time. Look to the past and ask what led to this situation? Ask how it is changing right now and look to the future to imagine what that might hold. What are the relationships between the different elements and perspectives? Are you seeing the dynamic interplay between them? How does change in one area impact another? Which aspects sit in opposition to each other? These questions are called 'mind openers' by cognitive scientist Otto Laske and consultant Jan De Visch.[14] They will help you to navigate your thinking around the different dimensions of an issue to enable a more systemic understanding.

Remember Tony, the disgruntled engineering team leader I introduced earlier (page 44)? The breakthrough for him (and his team) occurred when I set up a series of meetings with his boss, and most importantly his boss's boss. This process brought these multiple perspectives to life, not as 'thought experiments' but as real conversations. For the first time, Tony started to appreciate the bigger political and social factors that impacted the local authority. He realised that his was not the only department to be under pressure, and that 'they' were not out to get him. Importantly, his boss's boss, also started to understand for the first time what it felt like to be at this particular 'front line.' Shifting perspectives opened new and more constructive communication channels that helped Tony and his team become more engaged and empowered.

Thinking with others

Thinking well with others requires additional considerations to the approaches we have just discussed. The first is to create safety in the group, recalling that perceived threats will tend to lead to narrow, defensive thinking. Some simple ground-rules can help. Hold back on critiquing an idea until you are sure you understand it. Try to build on an idea by first responding with three things you like, then expressing any concerns as a wish for improvement. Give everyone time to think and write down their ideas before inviting contributions or brainstorming.

One barrier that commonly interferes with effective communal thinking is the desire to prove that you are the smartest person in the room. This is a particular risk for clever people, who will often quickly jump to a solution, then spend the rest of the meeting trying to convince everyone else of its merits. I refer to this as trying to sell your own cake to the team, rather than baking a cake together. If it is important to have buy-in to a course of action, you are often better off asking the right questions rather than coming up with the right answer. Timely questions can help the group stay on track, identify and challenge assumptions, and generate more ideas.

Conclusion

We are blessed with amazing gifts of intellect, reasoning and memory. Our brains hold more neurons and connections than stars in the galaxy, providing us with the means to create, invent, connect and choose. By learning to create a healthy, safe environment, developing the self-awareness to reflect on, and improve how we think, we can give ourselves the best chance to use these capacities most effectively for the greater good.

Want to work on this?

In Chapter 3 I showed how making the correct small, 1% changes can be a powerful lever for improvement. Here are three habits that can help you develop your capacity to think straight. Each one follows the 'habit change formula' – there is a trigger which is a specific event, time or location, and there is a new behaviour to replace what you currently do. Consider which of these changes would bring you the greatest benefit, one that has the most positive energy for you. Choose this one and work with it for a month, keeping a note of your progress each day. Record how and when you applied the new behaviour, and if you didn't manage the change, reflect on why not.

- When faced with a problem, instead of jumping to a solution, I will pause and challenge myself to think about it from a different perspective.
- When I am under pressure, instead of responding automatically, I will check whether I am 'above or below the line.'
- When I notice myself judging a situation or another person, instead of assuming I am right, I will ask 'How might I be wrong?'

Want to learn more?

A great online resource that offers resources, examples and references that support better thinking is the Farnham Street blog: https://fs.blog

I also recommend the book *Your Mind at Work* by David Rock (Harper Business, 2009). He provides lots of great recommendations that will help you think better and be more productive.

---

[1] Sternberg, R.J, Grigorenko, E.L. (2004).

[2] Rock, D. (2009).

[3] Heffernan, M. (2009).

[4] For discussion on Dysrationalia, see:
https://talentdevelop.com/2279/dysrationalia-defects-in-real-world-intelligence/,
and *https://www.bps.org.uk/psychologist/what-intelligence-tests-miss*

[5] More on the implications of Confirmation Bias is available at
https://catalogofbias.org/biases/confirmation-bias/

[6] To read more on Groupthink, see
https://www.psychologytoday.com/gb/basics/groupthink,

[7] Smith, M. (1998).

[8] Anthony, S.D. (2016).

[9] One of the best descriptions of this framework can be found here
https://conscious.is/video/locating-yourself-a-key-to-conscious-leadership

[10] De Bono, E. (1991).

[11] Kriegel, R. & Brandt, D. (1997).

[12] Van Oech, R. (2008).

[13] This technique of taking different positions was formalised as Perceptual Positions by NLP founders John Grinder and Richard Bandler in the 1980's but its roots are much older.

[14] De Visch, J. & Laske, O. (2020).

Chapter 5. Relate well

In this chapter I will focus on the critical role of human relationships for wellbeing and productivity. I will explain how and why relationships often suffer in a typical working environment and offer practical guidance on what you can do to communicate and engage better with your colleagues.

Summary

- Effective relationships provide for important human needs.
- Modern working practices often lead us to engage with each other as 'objects' or 'resources' not people.
- The capacity to switch focus from self to other is essential.
- Needs within a relationship have two key dimensions; task and personal, and both require recognition and attention.
- It is important to refine the use of language to foster better relationships.

Why relationships matter

Humans are social animals, and we have evolved to survive and thrive within a tribe. In indigenous Australian traditions, the worst crimes were punished not by death, but by out-casting and being made invisible to the tribe. In our society too we need human contact to survive, and because these needs have carried such weight over the millennia of human existence, our relationships can carry a great burden even now. They can be a source of joy, learning and love – and also of conflict, frustration and pain. The quality of working relationships is a critical factor for healthy high performance at work, and for satisfying and fulfilling family experience too. Research has shown that quality relationships are critical to wellbeing throughout our whole lives[1]. Performance without attention to right relationships comes at a cost and can feel like driving a bulldozer through a team. Yet relating purely for its own sake runs the risk of creating an unproductive and cosy environment where nothing much gets done.

If we are going to create a healthy way of working together, then we need to foster the conditions that meet our needs for connection and community. Real influence comes not just from job titles, but by the ability to activate human energy through a web of inter-connected relationships.

How modern work and our minds distort relationships

Many of the people I work with in organisations experience a typical working day as a steady stream of tasks; feeling swamped by hundreds of emails, back-to-back video meetings, with hardly time to pause for breath. Whilst company values often include exhortations to 'put people first' and engagement surveys ask if you 'have a best friend at work', the harsh reality is that attention to tasks and targets usually trumps people and relationships. Company culture combines with human psychology to further limit the quality of human interaction. Under these sorts of external pressures our brains respond by going into survival mode. This is a defensive psychological state in which two key shifts occur.

First, we lose empathy for others and see them as not as people but as objects, either useful to us or as barriers to achieving our own objectives. In this state we forget that others have their own experience and emotions. The most extreme version of this effect occurs when soldiers are trained to see their opponents as a faceless 'enemy', or as 'targets'.[2] This shift in perspective is essential if they are to carry out their orders. Very few of us would be willing to pull the trigger if we were fully aware of the real human being at the end of the scope. The terrible tragedy of post-traumatic stress injury in ex-servicemen[3] suggests that despite the indoctrination, many soldiers are aware of the true nature of war. Thankfully life in organisations is less extreme, but the pattern remains that we can all too easily objectify others. I recently heard a senior manager describe a difficult situation in which no humans were named; HR did this, Audit did that, Compliance did the other. When I invited a re-telling of the story using the names of the people rather than their job titles, there was a visible shift in my client's facial expression. "What's different now?" I asked. "Oh, I can see that they had pressures on them too, it must have been difficult for them, and they weren't just out to get us." The appreciation that there were people, not just functions, involved, shifted her understanding to a new and far more productive level.

The second psychological shift is related to the first. When I lose empathy for the other person I also move to a self-justifying state of mind, in which I blame the other person for the problem rather than taking personal responsibility to acknowledge my own contribution.[4] In this state I see myself and my behaviour as fully justified because of what the other person did or did not do. This pattern can be seen on a large scale in any long running conflict. One side might believe its military attacks are fully justified because of the threat of attacks from the other side, leading to needless loss of life and collateral damage. This pattern shows up in much more familiar environments too. In fact, the pattern can be particularly insidious in close relationships. To share a personal example, at times I hear my wife comment on the state of tidiness of our house. I can hear her request for my contribution to tidy up as a personal criticism, to which my mind responds by self-justification and blame. So, my triggered internal dialogue goes something like "What's she complaining about now? Doesn't she know that I took the garbage out yesterday? She's too fussy about the house and should just chill out, anyway I have been busy...". As a result, I will grudgingly respond with a sense of resentment at being dragged away from my work. Like many households, the objective reality is that she pulls more than her share of the weight on domestic duties. This is an uncomfortable truth for me to face. To protect myself, I lose empathy for my wife, forgetting that she too is busy and tired. I default to only seeing and defending my position, turning my own uncomfortable emotions toward her.

Losing empathy for others and self-justifying are normal human responses, made worse by a pressured and task driven working environment. What can we do about them? The answer lies within each of us, and as always, starts with self-awareness.

Self-awareness

Self-awareness is essential and underpins your ability to manage healthy and robust relationships. This may come as a surprise to those of us who have struggled with a difficult or conflicted relationship, where it often feels like the other person's behaviour is the cause of the problems. And, of course, the other person in the relationship is relevant, but rather than rushing to change or fix them, the first step is to look in the mirror. Paradoxically, you cannot be fully aware of another person if you are not fully aware of yourself. We are going to look at two important dimensions of self-awareness that directly impact your capacity to engage in constructive relationships. The first is the ability to shift your psychological focus between yourself and others, the second is awareness of your own needs.

Self and other

Your capacity to build and maintain healthy, effective relationships depends on your ability to navigate between a psychological focus on yourself and a focus on the other person. This is an extension of the perspective shifting skill I introduced in the previous chapter. Not everyone is versatile in moving between these states of mind. We can all think of people who cannot to go beyond their own self-interest, which in extreme cases is called narcissism. And you may have encountered people who have little or no sense of themselves, seeming to always rely on others for direction and validation.

I have seen the challenge of switching focus from self to other most clearly in a sporting context when a talented athlete retires and moves to a coaching role. Successful competitors are usually most comfortable focusing on themselves, and indeed it is one hallmark of a serious and committed athlete. Often, they can struggle at the start of a coaching career because they are not used to placing the well-being and performance of others first. Likewise, in the workplace a good manager needs to learn when and how to prioritise his or her team, or the good of the business, over self-interest.

Being able to de-centre and move to an understanding of, and empathy for, another person is an essential step to experiencing mutuality in relationships. Mutuality means that you recognise that the quality and effectiveness of a relationship is a shared responsibility – rather than something either of you is solely responsible for. Stepping into someone else's world is hard, but Stephen Covey's advice for highly successful people remains as important today as it ever was: "seek first to understand before being understood."[5] Learn to ask questions, withhold your judgement, and listen to the answers. Remember too that when you struggle to understand the behaviour or motivation of another person and feel like they are to blame, that "every villain is the hero of their own story". From the other person's perspective, they are behaving rationally and can justify everything they say and do. Just as you believe you are acting rationally from your perspective, so you may well appear to be the villain in their eyes! Whilst the other person's position may feel wrong or unhelpful, it is important that you do your best to understand (if not agree with) their perspective.

I saw this process produce powerful results when I was asked to mediate between two team members who were in serious conflict.

Tensions were running high between the manager and the leader of one of his teams, with frequent arguments, and even threats of violence. I met each of them individually first to understand what was going on. Mark, the recently appointed manager, was in his early forties. Well spoken, with an upright bearing and a precise manner, I wasn't surprised to learn that after attending public school he had joined the navy, rising to become a junior officer. Seeking a more settled family life, he left the navy after fifteen years and was now in charge of the regional emergency response function for a government agency. The bane of his life was his team leader, Ray. Mark described Ray as 'bolshie' and complained that he struggled to follow proper processes and was dismissive of direction.

I then met Ray, who explained that in his view, Mark was rigid and inflexible, wouldn't listen, and insisted on sticking to the rules even when they did not make sense or there was a faster way of working. Ray was a similar age to Mark, and still retained his cockney accent. He had left school at 15, struggled to find a job and joined the Royal Marines at 16, where he served for 20 years as a commando, reaching the rank of sergeant. I asked Ray how much he knew about Mark's background. "Not much, we have never really talked much about personal stuff."

Both Mark and Ray were stressed and struggling to step out of their own story. Each was the hero, feeling justified for their behaviour, and saw the other as the villain. I decided to set up a different conversation. I asked them each if they would be willing to meet the next morning, but not in the office. I suggested a local nature reserve, wanting to change the pattern of their normal interaction, and hopeful that some fresh air and a natural environment would help. I arrived at 8.30 am the next day, feeling a little anxious. Ray had been overheard to threaten that he would 'like to shoot the bastard' so I felt the stakes were high. The three of us gathered in the car park and walked a short distance to a park bench. It was a crisp, bright morning, and the views were expansive. I began "I have met each of you separately and heard your complaints about the other person. You have each also shared a little of your own history, and how you came to be in the jobs you are doing now. You have both told me you would like the situation to improve, because it is not a lot of fun for either of you right

THE WORK REVOLUTION

now. I do not know what the best solution is, and in any case that's for you to work out. But I do have a strong sense that it will be helpful for you to understand each other better. Are you willing to share your stories, and more importantly, to really listen to each other?" Both nodded in agreement. "Ray, would you begin, and tell Mark your story?" Mark listened and to his credit did not interrupt, as Ray, with only an occasional prompt from me, told his story: Growing up in a working-class family with a tough childhood. Struggled at school with undiagnosed dyslexia. Joined the Marines on the spur of the moment after seeing a recruiting poster. The Marines gave him, for the first time in his life, a feeling of self-respect and acceptance. A tough, challenging environment, where loyalty to your close-knit squad was paramount. Success in the field came from being agile, adaptable, fast moving in response to an unpredictable and hostile environment.

Then it was Mark's turn: An only child, comfortable middle-class childhood and enough social capital to attend a minor public school then university. Joining the Navy and gaining a commission, enjoying the structure and discipline of the naval hierarchy. Serving as a lieutenant on destroyer, with responsibility for communications. A destroyer, like any modern warship, is a complex combination of machinery and people. Orders from the bridge need to be translated quickly into action, using clear and consistent protocols and processes. There is no room for mavericks or independent action.

I could tell that much of what they were hearing about each other was new and I sensed a grudging, but growing appreciation for what they had each experienced and achieved in life. I reflected what I too had heard, in particular the way their different environments in the services had shaped their views of leadership. "So, is your current situation anything like being in the field as part of a commando squad, or being aboard a destroyer?" They both sheepishly nodded no. "So how come you are both behaving as if it is?" With some hesitation, they began to speak together, opening up about their frustrations, but also their hopes for a better working relationship. We spent the rest of the morning on the hill, as they continued to explore each other's motives and working preferences, and they began to map out a new way of working together. When I called them both about six weeks later, I learned that, while they hadn't become the best of friends, Mark and Ray had settled into a new and effective working relationship.

Understanding needs in relationships

You can't always get what you want
But if you try sometimes you might find
You get what you need
Mick Jagger and Keith Richards

The Rolling Stones were onto something important with these lyrics. Understanding your own, and other's needs creates the foundation for an effective relationship, whether at work or in the family. Needs within a relationship have two key dimensions: task and personal.

Task needs refer to the tangible actions or outcomes ensuing from the relationship. Sometimes this is simple. I need a shot of caffeine to jolt my brain into action, so I go to a café, order and pay for a coffee. The barista makes me a coffee. Our relationship is straightforward and goes no deeper than exchanging pleasantries. The tasks and expectations are clearly defined – my money in exchange for a decent cup of coffee – and so the relationship works fine.

In most working relationships the tasks, and the resulting transactions within the relationship, are more complex. A Sales Manager needs his Sales Representative to turn up on time, provide regular updates, and deliver the agreed results. The Sales Representative needs her manager to give clear direction, provide feedback, and to co-ordinate the input from other parts of the business. The Sales Manager agrees targets with the Sales Representative and receives weekly progress updates. If the targets are met, the Sales Representative gets rewarded.

In a working context like this, well designed and well understood job roles are the key to individual performance and smooth relationships because they will map out each person's responsibilities and expectations. Both Sales Manager and Sales Representative know what tasks they are responsible for delivering and what outcomes they are accountable for achieving. Roles tend to evolve and creep as demands change, so it is important to revisit and re-negotiate role definitions regularly. Job roles enable discussions about the tasks and inter-dependencies in working relationships to happen more easily. By taking the personal aspects out of the equation it is easier to talk about the behaviours and deliverables needed within a relationship. But no matter how clearly defined, job roles are not the same as the people filling them. This is why the second dimension of relationships matters.

Personal needs in a relationship refer to the human and emotional experience of the people in the relationship. One of the reasons that relationships become complicated or conflicted yet are also rewarding and enriching is that they are the vehicle for meeting these personal needs. If we add the personal needs to the example above, we see that:

Amir, in his role of Sales Manager, needs Sales Representative Harriet to respect his status and role.

Harriet, in her role of Sales Representative, needs Amir to be fair and to feel in control of her workload.

Personal needs can be harder to identify and acknowledge than task needs but they are just as important to the health of the relationship.

Typical personal needs in a relationship include:

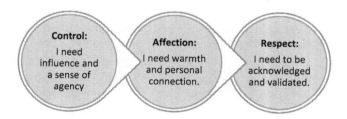

The importance of each of these needs will vary from person to person. As we saw in Chapter 1, the relative strength of these needs is shaped by a combination of inheritance and upbringing. The importance will also vary from relationship to relationship – the level of affection I seek from the barista who serves me coffee is (hopefully) different from the affection I seek from my wife. The final factor is the difference between the way I express a need in a relationship, and the amount I want from the other person. I may want the other person to show me respect, without it being equally important to me that I show respect in return.

In a healthy environment, people understand and accept that within a working relationship task and personal needs are subject to a negotiated agreement, not demands or impositions made of each other. When each person in a relationship is clear about their own needs and expectations and is willing to do their best to meet the other person's needs too, the foundation is in place for high performance.

This does, however, rely on several assumptions. First, that I am sufficiently self-aware to know what my personal needs are. Can I acknowledge that I need validation, control or affection? What if expressing this need feels like admitting a weakness or vulnerability? It can be tempting to try to ignore or downplay these factors and just 'get on with the job.' But emotions tend to come back stronger if ignored, and healthy relationships provide the space for this type of discussion.

For example, my business partner William and I need different levels of personal contact. I am quite self-contained, while William thrives on interaction. This means that he is more likely to pick up the phone than I am, and while I always enjoy our conversations, I initiate them less often. Because we have talked about this pattern and acknowledged our different 'settings', we can more easily manage what could have been seen as 'too many interruptions' by me, or as 'he is avoiding me' by William.

Second, and somewhat in contradiction to the first point, is it appropriate that I seek to meet all my personal needs within a working relationship? This is called 'managing boundaries.' Just because I feel a high need for affection, this does not mean I should expect affection from my work colleagues – or the person serving my coffee. Relationship boundaries get blurred all too often when people seek to meet their personal needs inappropriately. The results may be as innocuous as over-sharing personal concerns, through to becoming romantically involved with a work colleague, or at worst lead to workplace bullying which is a sign of a severely misplaced need for power and control. There seem to be generational differences about how to manage relationship boundaries. Millennials who have grown up with social media appear (at least to those of older generations) to have a much more porous boundary between personal and work relationships. This can lead to a mismanagement of expectations in a working relationship – what one person feels is a normal exchange between work colleagues can be embarrassing over-sharing to another.

How to improve relationships

In many relationships, whether at work or home, both task and personal needs are often assumed, unspoken, vague, or have changed over time. It is all too easy to fall into the mind-reading trap, in which I believe that what I need is so obvious that 'of course' the other person must know it. Tension in a working relationship is often due to the basic task transactions being misunderstood or inconsistently delivered. The solution is to regularly check in with colleagues and talk about your relationship. Most people find this uncomfortable to do, because it invites you to move from the task to the personal domain.

Here is a framework that can help by providing a simple structure for a conversation.

THE TEMPERATURE READING (ADAPTED FROM VIRGINIA SATIR)[6]
This framework helps communication within a variety of relationships, including partners, family or work colleagues. It consists of a short conversation in which each person takes it in turns to speak within the following structure:

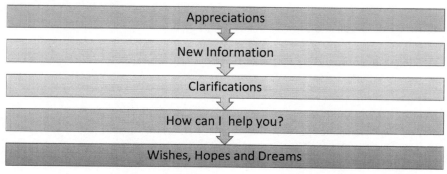

It will take about 20 – 30 minutes for a pair to work through this conversation, and you may find it easier to work with a coach or neutral colleague, who can guide you both through this list of headings. Here is how this conversation might unfold between Amir and Harriet. Recall that their relationship is strained because Amir, as a new manager, finds it difficult to give his more experienced team member Harriet feedback about her underperformance.

APPRECIATIONS
Relationships need regular inputs of appreciation; in the same way a well-designed engine still needs oil. Expressing appreciation helps to meet the human need for recognition, it expresses gratitude and reinforces what's

working well. This creates a humanised performance environment, with more goodwill and less defensiveness. Appreciation is not necessarily the same as liking or approving of the other's behaviour. For example, I can appreciate a colleague's drive and urgency, and still dislike the pressure this creates for me.

> **Amir:** "I appreciate that you have got lots of experience and you have been doing this job longer than me."

> **Harriet:** "I appreciate that you are trying to do get us on board with the new sales targets."

Amir is taking a bit of a risk here and shows some vulnerability. Harriet is a little surprised, so responds by being more positive about Amir than she expected to be.

NEW INFORMATION

The idea that we should park our personal lives at the door each morning contributes to the illusion that our identity is limited to our professional role. Deeper, more human relationships develop best when we share a little about what is going on in our lives.

Feeling encouraged by Harriet's response, Amir shares something about his life outside work.

> "My parents are thinking about selling up and moving to a smaller house, and that means I am going to find my own place sooner than I expected."

Harriet decides to take a risk too, by sharing news that she feels uncomfortable about, even a little ashamed that it puts her in a bad light as a parent.

> "I have been under pressure at home, my teenage daughter is struggling because she is getting bullied at school and we don't really know how to help. It's really keeping me and my husband awake at night"

This is a surprise to Amir, as he did not know much about Harriet's family. The knowledge that she might be distracted by these challenges is starting to create a new context for understanding her recent behaviour.

CLARIFICATIONS

If there are things you do not understand about a colleague, ask for clarification rather than fall into the mind-reading trap and assuming an answer. Asking for information also shows a commitment to clearing up misunderstandings and anxieties.

Amir decides it is time to start exploring the issue about Harriet's performance that he has been unable to address successfully.

"How do you feel about the new sales targets that have come down from head office?"

"Not great to be honest. They don't feel fair to me, and I cannot understand why they haven't stuck to the old system."

This leads to a new conversation that allows Amir to share more of the background to the new system, and for Harriet to explain how the changes are impacting her. Up to now, Amir had assumed he had explained this clearly to his team. But he hadn't taken the time to speak to each one individually and assumed everyone was happy.

HOW CAN I HELP YOU?

I have stressed both the role of personal and task in a relationship and also the importance of moving from a self to other orientation. Putting these two principles together leads to the immensely powerful questions: How can I help you? What do you need from me? How can I help you meet your task and (legitimate) personal needs?

"So, while you are dealing with your daughter being bullied, how can I help you?"

> "I'd like to reduce my targets over the next three months, and then backload the rest of the year so I can take a bit more time for my family. I need to feel that there's some give and take and that the new system is fair."

By responding to this question (and remember this is a mutual process, so both parties get to have a say) Harriet is describing what she believes will enable her to perform and be at her best. Expressing a clear need is a powerful form of feedback, that is very different from the usual notion of 'constructive feedback'. A need is not a judgement, it is a request about what you would like the other person to start doing, stop doing, do more or do less. There is no guarantee that your recommendation will be accepted. But it is an important first step in airing and resolving an issue.

> "Ok, we can look at your overall annual targets and adjust the next few months."

> "Thank you – and what do you need from me?"

> "I need you to be more supportive of me and my role and the new sales process when we are with the team. If you have a concern, please come to me directly rather than talk to the rest of the team without me."

Only agree to changes that you can deliver. If you say you will do something within a relationship it is important to do your best to live up to your commitment, and if you cannot for any reason, you need to be pro-active and raise this with the other person to apologise, take responsibility and, perhaps, re-negotiate. Trust is rapidly eroded when we experience failed expectations.

WISHES, HOPES AND DREAMS

We all have differing expectations and aspirations. Sharing goals openly, allowing ourselves to articulate our visions and dreams, gives energy and purpose to our teams and relationships.

> "I want this team to do well and smash our targets, I want us to be known as the best in the whole division."

> "Yes, that would be great. But to be honest, right now I am more concerned about helping my daughter!"

The Temperature Check provides a framework for Amir and Harriet to talk together in a different and more constructive way than before. It is especially useful for people working from the conformist and expert worldviews (see Chapter 3) because it helps tease out their professional and personal identities and needs.

High performance communication

Let's shift our view on relationships from an inner-directed focus on emotional and task needs and boundaries, to consider what behaviours are necessary to communicate most effectively with other people. I find the following map[7] an invaluable guide to communication and often share it with my coaching clients. It helps by increasing your awareness of the patterns within a conversation and opens new possibilities for changing HOW you relate and communicate for greater clarity, shared understanding, and action. Pretty much any substantial comment in a conversation is covered by one of these four categories:

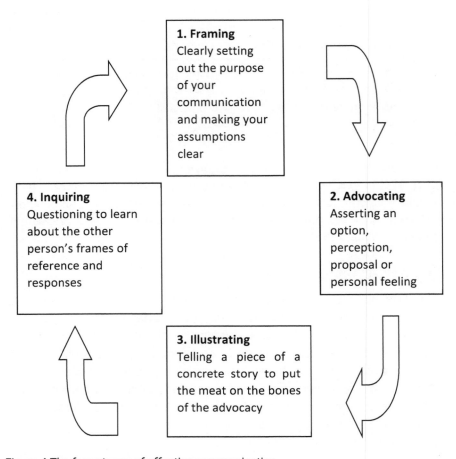

Figure 4 The four stages of effective communication

FRAMING

Framing occurs when I set the scene for what I want to say by explaining the purpose and context and laying out my assumptions. This orients the other person's attention to the topic and prevents either of us jumping to wrong conclusions. We can then share and test our interpretation of the situation.

How?

Headline your message: Do not go into too much detail, describe what you want to talk about and why it is important.

Reframe if necessary: If a discussion is losing focus or off track check the level of agreement and set a new context if necessary.

Example

Let's apply this to James and Steve (see Chapter 3) as James starts to take small, safe steps to delegate more and challenge his big assumption about the perils of losing control.

"Steve, I'd like to talk about how we are managing our client meetings."

Framing is often overlooked, particularly when time is short, so often I can dive straight into advocacy:

ADVOCATING

Advocacy is any statement in which I give direction, assert an opinion, or share a personal feeling. It gives direction and impetus to communication and (ideally) moves toward a resolution. Many conflicted conversations occur when two or more people are stuck advocating at each other. Simply adding more weight, or repeating, a position over and over does not help if you are working from a different set of assumptions. A solution is to step back to Framing and explore where and how you have alignment at this level.

How?[8]

Be candid and clear about the facts, your interpretation of them, and your feelings.

Take ownership for your views by saying "I" not "we", "you", "one", "people", etc. By taking personal responsibility you make it easier for people to understand where your statements are coming from. It is a form of trickery to disguise your own beliefs by saying "lots of people are telling me we should..."

Say 'I would like' rather than 'You should...' or 'We should...' A statement beginning 'I would like...' clarifies your involvement and interests and is consistent with your earlier framing of the situation. A statement beginning 'You should...' assumes that your framing of the situation is right and devalues the other person's position. It may even lead to an argument.

Example

"I'd like you to take the lead on more of our client meetings. This won't be easy for me to let go, but I want to make a start."

ILLUSTRATING

Illustrating is any statement that provides an example, gives evidence, or tells a story. Used well, a powerful and relevant illustration will bring your proposal to life. Used poorly, a long, rambling or irrelevant example quickly drains energy and interest in a conversation. There is an important relationship between advocacy and illustration: Advocacy without Illustration may be seen as criticism or blame while Illustration without Advocacy lacks direction.

How?

Talk from personal experience. A relevant personal example will engage other people's attention more than a rambling, second hand example.

Describe do not judge. Judgement is a particular form of opinion, and especially when negative can evoke defensiveness and inhibit change. If you must judge, ensure you have Framed your opinion and explained why you are doing so (Advocacy).

Example

"You know I don't like surprises. But I want to pull out of meetings like the one last Thursday, when we got caught up in endless detail with Frank over the planning approvals. So long as you check in with me first on our no-go areas, I'd like you to manage these meetings yourself and then just let me know if there is anything out of scope that needs my approval."

INQUIRING

Asking good questions is perhaps the most important, yet under-valued, stage of effective communication. Inquiry allows you to learn about the other person's frames of reference – how are they thinking and feeling about the issue? It helps you both understand and develop points of view, and it engages the other person to share their views and enter the discussion.

How?

Make a statement before asking a question. A question without context is at best inefficient and at worst threatening. Whether you voice it or not, there is always a statement behind a question which can clarify the question and make a response much simpler.

Listen and re-state their response to ensure you have understood. If you have already moved onto the next point in your own thinking, you will never really hear the other person. Give them the attention they deserve and be open to their views. If you cannot restate what they have said, you did not listen in the first place.

Example

"I know this is a big change, and you may not believe it will last. How do you feel about it? What problems do you anticipate?"

Giving feedback – understanding impact and intent

Let's now explore how to give feedback, so that it is aligned with developing a healthy, high-performing workplace. This approach is grounded in an assumption that neither the person giving nor receiving the feedback is 'right'. After all, we are all 'the heroes of our own stories' and we invariably believe that our actions are justified and correct. However, even when your intent is positive, your impact on others can be different than you expected, or even damaging. We tend to judge other people's behaviour based on their impact. We tend to judge our own behaviour based on our intent.

This feedback framework helps you to explore and understand the difference between intent and impact.[9] Because it is based on being above the line and staying curious, rather than being below the line and judging or defending, it works well with difficult and contentious topics.

Situation

- Start by framing – describe the situation, be specific about when and where it occurred. A real example is more powerful than generalised perceptions.

Behaviour

- Illustrate the observable behaviour. Describe what you saw and heard. Do not interpret, judge, or assume you know what the other person was thinking.

Impact

- Describe what you thought or how you felt in reaction to the behaviour. "I felt…" followed by a single word, like frustrated, happy, confused, sad. Or "I thought that this was unhelpful" or "I did not know what to say next."

Intent

- Ask about the person's original intent. Inquiring enables both of you to understand the gap between intent and impact.

To bring this to life, let's bring back James and Steve a couple of weeks after their previous conversation. James is feeling proud of himself as he believes he is stuck to his commitment to delegate more. Steve's experience is somewhat different, and from his perspective not a lot has changed.

James begins:

> **James:** Steve, tell me how it's been going for you since we agreed that you would manage the planning approval meetings.

Steve faces a key choice – does he ignore his own frustrations at his boss's recent behaviour, or does he take a risk and speak up? Taking a deep breath, Steve responds, (Framing the situation)

> **Steve:** "Well, remember the meeting yesterday with Frank when we went through the final costs?"

James nods, of course he remembers the meeting. Just as he had remembered some crucial questions that needed to be addressed after he had briefed Steve for the call.

> "You'd asked me to manage it, then halfway through the Teams call you dialled in to ask Frank more questions, then you left the call after five minutes." *(Illustrating the behaviour)*
>
> "I was really thrown because I wasn't expecting you to be there, and I'd already positioned with Frank that I was leading from our side. The rest of the call I was feeling worried that you might appear again at any time, and I don't think Frank really took me seriously." *(Describing the impact)*

Steve's heart rate has gone up and he has started to sweat. He is worried that he has exposed his own weaknesses and at the same time annoyed his boss. James too can feel his emotions rising. But not because he is annoyed with Steve – he is annoyed with himself for failing to stick to his commitment. Steve pauses, not sure whether to continue. James looks at him and indicates, "go on".

Steve asks,

> "What was in your mind when you joined the call?" *(Inquiring into James' intent)*

This is the critical moment, and it is up to James to catch this opportunity for learning. One part of him is feeling indignant that Steve has the gall to ask a question like this. "Doesn't he know it's my ******* company and I'll join any ******* meeting I want!" But as he takes a deeper breath he remembers the conversations with his coach, the work to uncover his big assumptions about losing control, and his commitment to make a change.

> "Well, it occurred to me that we hadn't drilled down into possible interest rate changes, and I didn't want us to get caught out. But if I reflect on it now, even if that had come up, we have still got another review before we sign. I guess I felt a bit anxious about not being there myself."

With a wry smile, he continued,

> "I guess I have got a bit more work to do on letting go of control. What would be more useful for you next time?" *(Sharing his intent and inviting suggestions for alternative behaviour)*

Steve suggests,

> "How about we give ourselves a little bit longer for our briefing meeting? This would make it easier for us to pick up any loose ends and I can go into the meeting knowing that you're confident I am well prepared." *(Alternative impact)*

Rather than Steve's feedback being blame or a complaint, it has created a powerful opportunity for learning. Steve has learned that it can be OK to take a risk and speak openly with his boss. James has learned how easy it is to be caught by his big assumption and the negative impact this has on his team. And their relationship is stronger as a result too.

Conclusion

We have explored the importance of relationships for healthy, human high performance and the challenge to really see others as people under the pressure and demands of organisational life. As well as staying aware to our mind's self-protective biases, we need the practical skills to negotiate and balance task and personal needs. I believe this boils down to both parties being able to ask and answer two fundamental questions:

What do I appreciate about you?

What do I need from you?

Want to work on this?

Here are three 1% habits that can help you develop your capacity to relate well. Each one follows the 'habit change formula' – there is a trigger, an event, time or location, and there is a new behaviour to replace what you currently do. Choose one that matters to you and work with it for a month, noting your learning in a diary.

- When things are difficult with a colleague, instead of blaming them, I will remind myself that we are both human beings with individual strengths and weaknesses.
- When I feel misunderstood, instead of repeating myself, I will show that I have understood the other person's point of view before going any further.
- At least once a week, I will choose one of my important relationships and share something I appreciate about the other person and what I need to be at my best.

Want to learn more?

The work of the Arbinger Institute is first rate and I have drawn on this in describing the perils of the self-justifying state of mind, which they refer to as 'being in the box'. See their books *Leadership and Self Deception*, *Anatomy of Peace* and *The Outward Mindset*.

For a thorough guide to working with difficult or conflicted conversations and conflict, see *Crucial Conversations, tools for talking when stakes are high*. Kerry Patterson, Joseph Grenny, Ron McMillan and Al Switzer (McGraw Hill, 2002).

If you find yourself in a relationship where it seems particularly difficult to establish mutual needs, you might find useful guidance here - *Why is it always about you? The Seven Deadly Sins of Narcissism*. Sandy Hotchkiss (Free Press, 2003).

---

[1] Xu, X., Mishra, G.D., Holt-Lunstad, J. and Jones, M. (2023).
Harvard Health Publishing (2010) *https://www.health.harvard.edu/staying-healthy/the-health-benefits-of-strong-relationships*
Brower , T. (2023).

[2] Discussion of soldiers trained in objectification, found in this article: *https://www.healio.com/news/psychiatry/20130621/jack_10_3928_1081_597x_201 30601_01_1205266*

[3] PTSD in soldiers:
https://www.ncbi.nlm.nih.gov/pmc/articles/PMC5047000/

[4] This pattern is described by C Terry Warner of the Arbinger Institute as being 'in the box.' Arbinger Institute (2010).

[5] Covey, S.R. (2020).

[6] Psychotherapists Virginia Satir and Lori Gordon are credited with this framework. You can find more here:
https://councilforrelationships.org/the-daily-temperature-reading-a-skill-for-life-long-love/

[7] I first found this in Rooke, D., Fisher, D., Torbert, W. R. (2003). They based it on work by Chris Argyris and Donald Schon.

[8] I learned these guidelines while working with John Syer. See Chapter 11 of Syer, J. & Connolly, C. (1996).

[9] https://www.ccl.org/articles/leading-effectively-articles/closing-the-gap-between-intent-vs-impact-sbii/

Chapter 6. Act powerfully

Having considered thinking and relating, now we come to taking action. In this chapter I will explain why it can feel so hard to get anything done, despite being busy all day. Then I will share practical steps you can take to make your environment more productive before introducing a powerful principle called the creative orientation.

Summary

- The typical digital working environment does not support real productivity.
- We often respond to this environment by seeking escape in distraction (flight) or compulsively overworking (fight).
- Putting constraints on using email and online time makes a positive difference.
- Productivity flows from a creative orientation in which we make clear choices about the results we want to create.
- Structural tension is a powerful force that arises when we hold current reality AND a desired result together in our mind.
- Mindfulness helps to develop your capacity to focus in a busy and distracting environment.
- Having a clear purpose increases focus and motivation.

Why action matters

"The difference between professional and amateur musicians is that amateurs perform beautifully when they feel inspired, while professionals perform beautifully no matter how they feel."

Robert Fritz: The Path of Least Resistance[1]

While I might argue that professionals produce even *better* music when they feel inspired, Fritz makes the important point that ultimately what counts is the performance; your actual behaviour, not how you feel about it. Action is the third part of the ART of Performance, and when done well it binds the intellect and the emotional connection in praxis – creating real change in the world. Action that is disconnected from thinking and relationships can appear bold and decisive yet is often experienced by others as that of a maverick. Insufficient commitment to action feels like being a back-seat driver, watching and advising others but never taking the wheel yourself.

Doing meaningful work is hugely motivating and given the number of hours we spend at work over a lifetime, it is essential for wellbeing that we spend our time as productively as we can. Sadly, productivity is often confused with busyness, or the passing of time in front of a computer screen, rather than in effectively and efficiently doing proper work. A healthy high performance environment is one in which you can achieve outcomes that make a real difference for customers, clients, or stakeholders – not simply 'be busy'.

Why modern work stops us getting much done

I am old enough to remember working in an office that did not have a single computer, where instead there was a typing pool in the corner where two women spent all day turning hand-written drafts into paper documents. Much of what they typed were standard letters, varying only in the name of the recipient and the amount of a government subsidy they were due to receive. Multiple copies of all correspondence were produced using carbon paper (ever wondered what CC meant when you copied an email?) with different coloured paper for different files. Business unfolded at a leisurely but effective pace as letters passed in the post over several days. Of course, there was the telephone, and nearly everyone had one on their desk. On one occasion I had to go two floors down to the Tax Office to ask them to fax an important document to Canberra – they were the only government department in a 12-story building to have one.

More than 40 years and one pandemic later it all feels very different. Companies employing knowledge workers have been forced to accept the reality that an office is no longer essential so long as you have a laptop and decent wi-fi. This new approach to work still seems strange, or improper to people from older generations. I recall, pre-pandemic, a senior director in his late fifties describe with outrage that his twenty-one-year-old son was able to do his job running an IT help desk while he lay at home in bed! Yet we now know that many people can do their job from anywhere.

As we learn to navigate a return to offices after COVID, we are re-evaluating what the office could or should be. Do we really want to return to open plan offices that have the look and feel of battery chicken farms, with rows of desks and screens extending into the distance? Where people created their own private space by using noise-cancelling headphones sat atop their head and ears like a sign saying, 'do not disturb'?

Even pre-pandemic we were hardly ever disconnected from the online world, courtesy of the multiple devices we use every day. Work follows us wherever we go, with the expectation that we will respond immediately no matter what time it is, where we are, or who we are with. Added to this, we are now our own travel agents, insurance brokers and bankers, courtesy of the new digital economy, so being 'at work' usually includes attending to a constant stream of online domestic tasks. I counted the number of ways I can be contacted online – by Zoom, Teams, text, via Facebook, WhatsApp, Telegram, Slack and email, all depending on the person or people in my network. In the face of this overwhelming sensory and information overload and attendant emotional discomfort we respond yet again with one of two main strategies: fight or flight.

The flight response leads to distraction, procrastination, and avoidance. Rather than doing real work or recognising that the work we are asked to do is meaningless, we seek solace, scrolling through the never-ending online world to find the dopamine fuelled rewards of red hearts and social media 'likes'. The addictive power of smartphones and screens is increasingly recognised, and as a friend with first-hand experience of serious addiction says, "they're worse than crack cocaine." Other avoidance strategies outside of work include binging on TV box sets, overeating and drinking too much.

The fight response drives us to throw ourselves into work without respite. 300 emails a day becomes a dragon to be slain by perseverance and late nights onscreen after the kids have gone to bed. Despite dropping off to sleep at 1 am to the blue glow of an iPad screen, the next working day starts in the office at 7am. Weekends blur into weekdays, marked only by a cursory attendance at a school football match, or nodding off early over dinner with friends. Sunday night is a source of dread, knowing that you will be awake at 3 am and already stressed about the week ahead. Emotional and physical burnout follows.

There are two clear elements: the external environment, and our internal, emotionally driven response. Let's start with some practical steps to improve your external conditions.

Organising your working environment

If you set out to create the worst possible conditions for focused and effective knowledge work, you would end up with a typical open plan office or unboundaried home working with constant online access. A study of 1000 office workers found that they were interrupted for an average of 2.1 hours per day, equivalent to nearly 30% of a 'normal' workday.[2] Another study discovered that office workers manage an average of just 11 minutes on a task before interruption – defined as a colleague stopping by, being called away or leaving the desk, incoming e-mail, switching tasks on a computer or a phone call.[3] The negative impact of this is called the 'task switching penalty.' Put simply, when we stop and start it takes longer to complete a task, and we make more errors, than when we complete a knowledge-based task in one block of attention. When we start a new task, two different brain systems are engaged. The first system shifts your attention to the new task, then another calls up the relevant 'rules' or operating principles. This takes time and energy, and if you do a lot of switching in the day it can add up to a loss of 15 – 40% of your productivity. Now that many of us work virtually a lot of the time, we are glued to screens all day and jumping from one video call to another without respite. So, if we recognise the problem and the cost, what's the solution?

There are several tactics that can help.

30 MINUTE BLOCKS

If you need to attend to a specific and important thinking task, do it in thirty-minute blocks. Commit to doing NOTHING in this time other than work on your task. Set a timer and then turn your devices onto flight mode for the duration. This instantly creates a useful barrier between you and the online world. At the end of the thirty minutes, take a break. Get up and move away from your screen, go outside, stretch, move. If you are working at home and have a garden, go there for your coffee break. This is far more effective than a two-minute break every ten minutes and gains you an additional hour of productive time each day.

TAKE CONTROL OF YOUR DIARY

I once asked an over-worked client "when do you schedule time in your diary to focus on your key priorities?" He seemed shocked at the idea and replied, "I don't, I spend my day going to meetings that other people have put in my diary, then I do my own work from 6 to 9 pm." No wonder his home life was suffering. Instead, I encouraged him to block out time and allocate it to specific tasks, including time to think, read and reflect. If you have an assistant who manages your diary, educate them about the need to preserve these times from encroachment. Virtual assistants like Microsoft Viva are increasingly popular, as a senior executive recently said to me with delight "it finds the empty space in my calendar and blocks it out!". Let your colleagues know too, to manage their expectations about when you are and aren't immediately available. Be clear about why you are attending any meeting – what's your specific contribution, and how will it add value for you, your colleagues, or your customers? Many people attend meetings out of habit, a fear of missing out, or a desire to 'show willing'. None of these are very good uses of your time and energy. Challenge why a meeting should last either 30 or 60 minutes. Change your default to 25 or 50 minutes so you have breathing space between video calls.

RETHINK HOW YOU DEAL WITH EMAIL

Rather than being a serial task that runs all day, experiment with processing your email as set of batched tasks that you attend to at specific times. Set aside several 30-minute blocks in the day when all you do is respond to emails and at other times turn off distracting notifications that ding or show a flag. When you have set aside time for focused work, shut down your email completely – you can even put an 'out of office' autoreply telling people when you will respond. Rather than start your working day by checking email or checking your social media feeds, experiment with taking the first 15 minutes to think about your own priorities and ensure you are well-prepared for upcoming meetings or events. Starting your day with email invariably means you will be reacting to someone else's priority rather than your own. Give yourself an email curfew in the evening too, commit to a specific 'last time' you will check emails and screens before going to bed. And please, leave your phone outside your bedroom! If you do choose to work on emails in the early morning or late evening, do not send them straight away. If you do, particularly if you are the boss of the recipient, you are sending a powerful signal that you work long hours, and the implicit expectation is that you want an immediate response. Unless the matter really is time critical, hit 'send' at a reasonable time the next morning or use the delayed send feature on your email client. Ask yourself will it *really* make a difference if the email is received at 8am tomorrow rather than 11pm tonight?

A related problem to email is the lure of smart phones and the online world. I do not claim any special immunity to this, and like most people when I have a spare moment my habitual response is to pull out my phone, check email, scroll through the news, browse social media and so on. Instead, cultivate the habit of always having a book 'on the go', that you can read when you have a spare moment instead of defaulting to your phone. Using a pen and paper notebook also works well – it seems more satisfying and generative to write ideas and thoughts down on a page instead of onto a screen.

I have experimented and applied all the tactics I have just described. They work, but none are a silver bullet, because the most important changes to becoming more effective happen on the inside. Unless we also make an essential change in our fundamental orientation to work, we will fall back into overwork or avoidance.

The creative orientation – overcoming barriers to action

Since I first encountered Robert Fritz's book, *The Path of Least Resistance,*[4] in 1989 and learned to apply its principles it has had a profound personal influence and been transformational for many of my clients. Whenever we act from fight (overwork) or flight (avoidance and distraction), we are living from what Fritz calls the reactive-responsive orientation. In this orientation, our behaviour is an attempt to change how we feel, because feelings of anxiety, uncertainty, worry, boredom and so on are unpleasant, uncomfortable, or even frightening. In the short term, overwork or avoidance provide immediate respite from uncomfortable emotions. But as we have seen, over time both patterns become deeply damaging, to ourselves and the people who work with us.

The alternative, in Fritz's view, is to develop a creative orientation. Living in a creative orientation involves becoming very clear about the results you want to bring about in your life, and consciously choosing them. Fundamental choices might include to be healthy, to be free, to do meaningful work or to have healthy relationships. Once you are clear about your fundamental, or primary choices, then it becomes much easier to prioritise your energy and activity though an ongoing series of secondary choices. I regularly witness this principle when I'm working with top athletes. Very few ever feel they are making sacrifices in their social lives in pursuit of excellence, they are more likely to say "I do not see it as a sacrifice, I am choosing to prioritise my sporting career." These choices are driven by an internal impetus rather than an emotional reaction to circumstances. I believe that what Fritz describes as moving from the reactive-responsive to creative orientations is another way of describing Kegan's evolution from the socialised to the self-authored forms of mind that we discussed in Chapter 2. And in terms of the healthy high performance thinking that we covered in Chapter 4, a creative orientation looks and feels a lot like being 'above the line' while the reactive – responsive orientation has much in common with being 'below the line.'

The creative principle is the same regardless of the scale of the endeavour, whether your chosen result is to finish a report, or to build a whole new business. In launching the US Apollo space mission in 1962, President Kennedy proclaimed, "we *choose* to go to the moon", not "we *should* go to the moon."[5] By framing this mission as a choice, he invoked a spirit of freedom and autonomy that led to a national outpouring of energy and innovation. The same principle applies when we move from doing something because we 'should' or 'have to', to doing it because we 'want' to. The key criteria for an effective result are that you can clearly envisage it, and it is something you are choosing to want. If these two statements are true, that is enough to be getting on with.

Structural tension

Growing up in Australia, a friend who was always talking about his grand plans but never did anything about them was nicknamed Gunna– because "he's gunna do this, then he's gunna do that." Likewise, many people I meet in organisations are rightly cynical, and even suspicious, about leaders who talk about wonderful visions of the future that are disconnected from today's reality. Sadly, corporate visions often become no more than a faded poster on the wall rather than anything real. So, aspiring to an outcome is only part of the creative process. Without connection to reality, a vision is just a dream. Yet to dwell only on the how things are now, without hope of change can leave us feeling stuck. Fritz addresses this conundrum by a mechanism he calls structural tension. This is the gap that exists between current reality (how things are now) and your vision (the results you want to create). By holding in mind both your current reality and your desired result, you naturally start to create a path towards the vision. This path may be clear and obvious or may seem long and tortuous. What matters is that you take the first step, because by taking action you begin to create momentum. Current reality then changes, no matter how subtly, and by regularly acknowledging the gap between current reality and your desired result, progress unfolds. As the poet David Whyte says:

"Start close in,
don't take the second step
or the third,
start with the first
thing
close in,
the step you don't want to take."[6]

Importantly, structural tension is not same as emotional tension, such as feeling anxious when you anticipate a difficult conversation, or guilty at not having behaved with integrity. Fritz instead likens structural tension to the force created when a rubber band is stretched between your hands. If one hand represents the result you want to create in the future, and the other hand represents your current reality, the natural movement is towards the result, provided we maintain that as the fixed point.

Friction

The Prussian General von Moltke revolutionised military strategy by ensuring that his troops on the ground remained clear about their objective and had the freedom to invent their own tactics to achieve it. He famously declared "no battle plan survives its first encounter with the enemy." Likewise, Fritz cautions against becoming too invested in a particular plan or process to reach your vision. Instead by frequently and honestly assessing current reality and testing against your vision (and creating structural tension) you remain open to helpful circumstance and fresh initiatives. Historian and management consultant Stephen Bungay applied von Moltke's insights to the challenge of action in the organisational domain. He makes a particularly useful observation about the impact of friction whenever we try to get something done. "Friction is a function of the finitude of the human condition – the fact that our knowledge is limited and the fact that we are individual agents."[7] Simply, in any endeavour there are many things that will get in the way and many things that will go wrong. Friction shows up when people interpret the same communication differently, when tasks take longer than expected, when people do not understand their part in the larger plan, when information is imperfect or wrong, and through unpredictable events and random chance. Rather than assuming we live in a perfect, frictionless world, it is far better to accept friction and indeed prepare for it without getting upset. Friction will always affect your progress and change current reality, but it does not have to change your vision.

Mindfulness and current reality – accepting what is

Current reality is an accurate, objective description of your current state. It includes your emotions, your thoughts, your physical state, and your circumstances. It can be surprisingly difficult to describe current reality, because the reactive-responsive orientation is an on-going attempt to deny it. Rather than acknowledging that "right now I feel bored" or "right now I am avoiding conflict", we deal with these uncomfortable feelings through distraction or immersion in work. And as we saw in Chapter 3, self-awareness is a skill that takes practice.

Learning to accept current reality is helped by the practice of mindful acceptance, an increasingly widespread application of ancient contemplative practices. In the words of one of its greatest contemporary proponents, Jon Kabat-Zin, mindfulness is "awareness that arises through non-judgementally paying attention, on purpose, in the present moment."[8]

Developing mindful acceptance is simple but not easy. Simple, because to practise requires no more than to sit quietly, close your eyes and bring your attention to your breathing. Not easy, because you will quickly realise that your mind is full of thoughts, both pleasant and worrisome, that will take your attention away into the past or the future before you know it. The act of mindfulness isn't reaching a blissful, spaced-out state of mind – it is the discipline of noticing a thought or emotion, without judgement, and gently and persistently bringing your attention back to the present moment. When practising, some people prefer to focus on repeating a short word or phrase (known as a mantra) instead of following their breath. There are many approaches, including listening to guided exercises, and I encourage you to experiment and find what works best for your personal preferences.

Do not confuse being mindful with being passive and low energy. When you sit quietly and pay attention to your breathing and physical body, a natural side effect is to feel calm and relaxed. Think of sessions like this as the equivalent of a gym session for your mental concentration. But the important thing that you are doing in this type of exercise is to train your attention, not just to chill out. It is possible to be present and mindful at any time, doing any activity. You can mindfully sprint 100 metres, go for a walk, work in the garden, or take a phone call. They key is that your attention is in the here and now, on the activity you are doing, fully accepting all your experience.

There are many benefits to developing and practising this discipline. Mindfulness helps to develop your capacity to focus in a busy and distracting environment. It reduces stress and anxiety and improves physical functioning, lowering blood pressure and reducing coronary risk. However, critics also point out that a mindful approach can easily slip into apathetic acceptance and compliance with an unfair or unjust system. As George Bernard Shaw said,

> *"The reasonable man adapts himself to the world: the unreasonable one persists in trying to adapt the world to himself. Therefore, all progress depends on the unreasonable man."*[9]

I believe that this criticism of mindfulness is answered through Fritz's approach of both fully accepting the reality of how things are right now (mindful acceptance) AND enlisting the powerful human capacity to envision a more positive future (Bernard Shaw's 'unreasonable man' – or person).

Bringing this to life

Let's move from a theoretical description to a real example, by considering how the same person might respond to a situation from both the creative and from the reactive-responsive orientations. We will enlist Laura, our hardworking young lawyer. She is working from home to complete an important client brief.

Reactive – Responsive Laura (notice how she goes below the line)

"Thank goodness I don't have to race to the station for the 6.30 train this morning, I can get up a bit later and catch up on that Netflix mini-series and still have time to make a start by 9 am." Sitting in front of the TV at 8.30, she thinks "That episode was brilliant, I will just stay on and sneak in the next one, I've got all day to get the work done". One episode blurs into another as she is immersed in an alternative world of drama and political intrigue. By 10.30 Laura is feeling uneasy. It has been fun to indulge herself and binge-watch, but she is increasingly aware that she hasn't achieved anything today. She imagines her clients feeling disappointed and expectant of her, and this feeds her sense of guilt, an emotion she does not much like. Deciding that it is time for a snack, she heads to the kitchen for a coffee and to finish off some left-

---

over chocolate pudding from the fridge. Despite the sugar and caffeine rush her inner dialogue becomes more critical – "You have wasted your time, you're so lazy" she tells herself, "I might as well just write off today, I haven't got time to finish my work properly now anyway. So what if the work's not done today? I will do it on the weekend instead. I have worked really hard for weeks, and I've not got any credit for that, so I deserve a day off." Feeling justified, and with her guilt now pushed well into the background, she returns to the sofa with a fresh coffee and the remainder of the pudding to hit 'play' on her tv remote. The rest of the day seems to disappear, despite a brief attempt to open her laptop which led to her answering a slew of emails – none of them anything to do with her priority work. At about 9 pm, after a somewhat irritable evening meal with her husband, Laura retreats to her study and works into the small hours to finish her report.

Creative Laura (notice how she stays above the line)

"Thank goodness I don't have to race to the station for the 6.30 train this morning, for once I have got time to go for a run before work." During her run in the park near her home, Laura lets her mind freewheel and enjoy the experience of moving in the outdoors, before she starts to think about the work she needs to finish today. She recalls her conversations with her clients; a family business in dispute with an insurance company that is holding up payment for a claim. Without the insurance money they are unable to refurbish their fire-damaged factory, so the business has come to a standstill, impacting the family, their fifteen employees, and their customers. Laura's work today will bring together the key elements of their case, and it really matters to them. It is the sort of case that Laura loves too, being on the side of the underdog fighting a big corporate insurance company. By 8.30 Laura is sitting at her desk, feeling invigorated after exercise, and re-fuelled by a bowl of porridge. Before opening her laptop, she reminds herself of the current state of her draft submission and forms a clear intent about what she wants to achieve today. She commits to three, 30-minute working blocks, after each one she will take a five-minute break, have a coffee and stretch her legs. At lunchtime Laura reflects on the progress she has made in her three working sessions of the morning and compares this to her intended outcome of the day. She figures that two more 30-minute blocks should be enough, and that if she can put in a couple of quality hours in the afternoon that will leave enough time to catch up with her favourite Netflix mini-series before her husband gets home. She is in a good mood at 6 pm, feeling satisfied about her day's work and ready to surprise her partner with the suggestion that they go out to a local restaurant for the evening.

Alignment, purpose and motivation

You will have noticed that Creative Laura knows why her work is important and that this plays a key role in her capacity to commit to it productively. Conversely, Reactive Responsive Laura has not made a clear connection between her immediate task and either her client's needs, her firm, or her own values. She easily slips below the line without this motivation.

"Depend upon it, sir, when a man knows he is to be hanged in a fortnight, it concentrates his mind wonderfully," said Samuel Johnson.[10]

Extreme perhaps, and imminent hanging is not a threat for most of us or for Laura, but this well-known quotation makes a valid point about the importance of importance. Knowing that something matters, that our work has meaning and impact, is a wonderful antidote to distraction. Furthermore, a sense of purpose can be a source of motivation and even inspiration. I often illustrate this by the following old, and probably apocryphal story:

> Once upon a time, a visitor was walking through a busy construction site. He paused before a labourer who was sweating in the hot sun. "What are you doing?" the visitor asked. The labourer paused, gave a glance and sharply replied "I'm laying bricks". The visitor nodded and walked on. He paused before another worker and asked, "what are you doing?" With a sense of pride this man answered, "I'm laying these bricks to build a wall." The visitor went a little further on to a third man and repeated his question, to which he received a beaming smile and the words "I am building a cathedral to the glory of God."

Each of the workers is laying bricks. They vary in their enjoyment and engagement because of how much their contribution *matters* to them. The worker who gives his role the greatest meaning and feels a sense of purpose is the most satisfied and engaged. Simon Sinek made the same point with his exhortation to 'start with the why, not the what.'[11] Having a clear sense of purpose, knowing why your work is important, and to whom, provides a powerful source of motivation that can underpin productive and focused engagement. Of course, a meaningful purpose alone is insufficient for an effective working environment. As anyone who has worked in the not for profit or charitable sectors will know it is quite possible to have a higher purpose *and* a toxic working culture at the same time. In some cases, the higher purpose is used to justify poor pay and working conditions because it is part of 'serving the cause.' One of the problems with modern work is that the purpose of most companies is simply to generate financial returns for shareholders. Hardly an inspiring cathedral and no wonder many people's sense of purpose goes no further than maximising their own financial situation. This is one of the key themes in the emerging world of 'B Corps' and conscious capitalism – inventing organisations with a meaningful purpose that simultaneously meet the needs of financial investors, employees and wider stakeholders.

Working out your purpose and core contribution may be easier said than done; which one of your 43 'priorities' is the most important? There is a simple tool called a strategy tree that can help you connect your daily activities with your bigger context, and at the same time help to prioritise your time and energy.

USING A STRATEGY TREE TO CONNECT YOUR WHY, WHAT AND HOW

Use post-it notes, and begin by writing down your main objectives, one per note. Consider each of these as a 'what.' For each task, ask yourself "why am I doing this?" write the answer on a new post-it note, and place it *above* the relevant objective. Repeat the process of asking why about each task and (hopefully) you will soon map out your key contributions to your team or company's strategy, purpose and vision. Then go back to the level of your key objectives and ask the question "how am I doing this?", and again, write the answers on post-it notes which you place *below* the objective. This line of questioning should take you into the specific actions that will deliver your objectives. Do not worry about covering everything you do, as you can quickly end up with dozens of post-its. Developing your ability to use 'why, what and how' logic helps you to quickly determine which of your activities are aligned to your core contribution and purpose, and which are peripheral. The exercise may also highlight a lack of alignment or fuzzy thinking elsewhere in your business, if you discover that objectives lead to contradictory or dead end 'whys'.

Conclusion

Modern technology and the digital world offer wonderful opportunities for connection and access to information that can fuel creativity and innovation, so long as we also put effective constraints in place to help us stay focused on achieving real outcomes. In this chapter we have discussed what you can do to make your work environment more productive, largely by becoming more disciplined in how you use email and work online.

Internally, the key step change in productivity comes when you move to a creative orientation and just as Robert Fritz says of professional musicians, learn to produce your version of 'beautiful music' because it is important and you choose to, rather than be limited by how you feel.[12] Of course, it helps to choose outcomes that are meaningful and purposeful.

In the next section, we will move on from an individual focus on how you think, relate and act to consider leadership that engages, influences, and supports other people.

Want to work on this?

Here are three 1% habits that can help you develop your capacity to act powerfully and get things done more effectively. Each one follows the 'habit change formula' – there is a trigger that is an event, time or location, and there is a new behaviour to replace what you currently do. Choose one that matters to you and work with it for a month.

- Each morning before I look at my smart phone or computer, I will take 5 minutes to think about my priorities and make clear choices about my day.
- When starting a task or project I will make sure I understand why and to whom it is important and choose to do my best for them.
- When I brush my teeth, I will do so mindfully and bring all my attention to the here and now.

Want to know more?

I have drawn heavily on Robert Fritz and recommend you read *The Path of Least Resistance*. The first edition is more concise than the second.

Likewise, I thoroughly recommend *The Art of Action: How leaders close the gaps between plans, actions and results* by Stephen Bungay (Nicholas Brealey Publishing, 2011).

If you really want to get into the nuts and bolts of productivity, Dave Allan offers lots of resources here: https://gettingthingsdone.com

---

[1] Fritz, R. (1989)

[2] Spira, J. B. & Feintuch, J. B. (2005)

[3] M. González, V. and Mark, G. (2004)

[4] Fritz, R, (1989)

[5] Kennedy, 1962 speech available at:
https://www.jfklibrary.org/learn/about-jfk/historic-speeches/address-at-rice-university-on-the-nations-space-effort

[6] Whyte, D. (2012)

[7] Bungay, S. (2011)

[8] Kabbat-Zinn, J. (2004)

[9] George Bernard Shaw (1903), *Man and Superman, Maxims for Revolutionists*, available at *http://www.quotationspage.com/quotes/George_Bernard_Shaw/*

[10] Samuel Johnson was an 18th century essayist known for many great quotes. *https://www.britannica.com/biography/Samuel-Johnson*

[11] You can find out more about Sinek's work and books here:
https://simonsinek.com/books/start-with-why/ and here
https://www.ted.com/talks/simon_sinek_how_great_leaders_inspire_action/comments

[12] Fritz, R. (1989)

Section 3.
Putting this all into practice

The real power of the ART of Performance comes not just from improving your own well-being, but from improving your capacity to influence others and create a healthy working environment. In this section I will show how these principles apply when we come together in teams. Then, I will share a new framework for leading the performance of other people and whole organisations.

Chapter 7. Building Exceptional Teams

Up to now, this book has been about you as an individual contributor at work. Now we change context and explore teams. I will describe how teams have changed and how they can play an essential role in healthy high performance. I will then share a practical guide to building and leading a team, that works at any scale of organisation.

Summary

- The nature of teams has changed over the last 25 years, operating in a more dynamic and unpredictable world.
- The Pandemic has accelerated this change and led to new challenges for remote and hybrid teams.
- Teams can provide belonging, leverage diversity, promote learning and foster change – provided several challenges are managed.
- Being an effective team member is aided by all the skills and approaches we have discussed so far.
- The Exceptional Teams framework is a pragmatic guide to building and leading your team.
- Sustainable motivation in a team is based on the 5 Cs: clarity, connection, confidence, control and challenge.

Why teams matter

Teams are fundamental to how we work and live. In organisations they are the engine-rooms of creativity, problem solving and production, they are the biggest levers of change, and at their best they are rich laboratories for our learning and growth. Outside of work we live in and rely on teams too, whether these are our families or flatmates, or the musicians, sportspeople, or club mates we spend time with. Yet few of us would say that teams are always easy, straightforward or places of pure joy. Some of us will run a mile from teams and choose to work alone whenever possible. Sadly, teams can be toxic, dysfunctional, and even dangerous. This is inevitable given how easily our ego driven behaviour can get out of control. Clearly, if we are going to create workplaces where people can thrive, grow and accomplish, we need to understand how to lead, and be members of, healthy and high performing teams. These are teams where people can contribute all their talents, collaborate with their peers in a spirit of mutual accountability and shared responsibility, with high levels of trust and positive energy. As Simon Sinek said, "A team is not a group of people that work together. A team is a group of people that trust each other."[1]

How teams are changing

My first experience of being in a team started at the age of 10 when I joined the Scouts and found myself allocated to a Patrol, a group of five or six boys who worked together in various activities. Nominative determinism was strangely powerful – Beaver patrol was conscientious while the Devils patrol were always the troublemakers. I was in Wombats, so make of that what you will. Once in a Patrol you stayed there. When I started work in an office in 1982 it was the same, there was a clear hierarchy, team membership did not change often other than through promotion, and the idea of being in more than one team at any time was unheard of.

As I have worked with organisational teams over the last thirty years, I have seen teams change, due to the impact of the globalisation and the increased speed of digital connectivity. This change first came into focus in the mid-90s when I worked with several Jaguar car project teams. At the time, Jaguar was owned by Ford Motor Company, and it was a period of significant challenge for Jaguar employees. They were learning to work in matrix project teams to design and build more complex cars, quicker and more cheaply (and despite what the Jaguar purists said, the new cars also broke down less). Ford Motor Company was investing heavily in Total Quality Management (TQM) which relied on teams for successful implementation. This has been followed by methodologies such as Six Sigma, Lean Manufacturing and Agile that have all placed cross functional project teams at the heart of quality improvement and rapid product development processes.[2]

Broadly, we have seen teams shift in the following ways since the mid-1990s:

From	To
Relatively enduring and stable	Fluid and transient
Being a member of one or few teams	Being a member of many teams
Usually co-located in a physical space	Wide geographical spread and virtual
All employed by the same company	A mix of employees, contractors, consultants and clients.
Shared culture and working assumptions	Diverse culture and working assumptions
Single point of leadership	Flat or distributed leadership
Communicating mainly in person and through a limited range of channels	Communicating mainly digitally/ virtually through a wide range of channels
Sitting within a hierarchical organisational structure	A node in a complex network of teams
Relatively few external dependencies and stakeholders	Multiple and changing external dependencies and stakeholders
Operating in a generally stable, predictable external context	Operating in a **V**olatile, **U**ncertain, **C**omplex and **A**mbiguous context

This does not mean that today all teams are operating exclusively in the right-hand column. There are still plenty of examples of stable, hierarchical teams, such as senior leadership teams or service delivery and execution focused teams, but increasingly people find themselves working in project or development teams. These more fluid teams may last only days or a few weeks, or form and reform through the year as the business cycle evolves. Teams are no longer geographically constrained, and it is now common for teams to include people from multiple geographies and cultures. This trajectory was massively accelerated in 2020 with the impact of COVID-19, which practically overnight forced companies to fully adopt remote working and virtual meeting technologies. If companies are to thrive in this context, they need to establish a culture that encourages and enables effective and agile teamwork.

Harnessing the power of teams

Why are teams so important and what are the key challenges to unlocking their contribution? I see at least four interconnected paradoxes:

TEAMS PROVIDE SOCIAL CONNECTION AND BELONGING

As we have seen in the opening chapter, human behaviour is driven by a mix of nature and nurture, in which each of us seeks to meet our core human needs – such as belonging, control or achievement. We are social animals, primed to belong to a group and fearing exclusion. Our ancient ancestors who learned to collaborate survived and passed their genes on to us. Going it alone usually led to NOT surviving, so the people who cooperated with others were more likely to survive and pass on their genes. At their best, teams offer inclusion and belonging.

And yet...

For as long as humans have been in tribes, emotional tussles over belonging and control have played out in teams. Put a bunch of people together and we immediately see some striving to meet their emotional needs and acting in ways that are variously productive, frustrating, or entertaining. That is why 'reality' TV shows like *Love Island* and *I'm a Celebrity* are so popular, because they offer a safe window into the messy world of group relationships. But groups like these differ from teams. According one of the most widely accepted definitions of a team from academics Katzenbach and Smith, "a team is a small number of people with complementary skills who are committed to a common purpose, set of performance goals, and approach for which they hold themselves mutually accountable."[3] Behaviour that might be entertaining when watching a group of strangers interact in a TV show becomes deeply problematic when it occurs in a team striving to achieve shared results.

TEAMS CAN BRING TOGETHER DIVERSE TALENTS
One of the most consistent research findings into teamwork is that diverse teams are more effective than teams comprised of very similar people.[4] Diversity is not just a matter of gender – although this is often the most obvious dimension. Team members can differ in their culture of origin, their life experiences, their ways of thinking and professional expertise. There is an increasing awareness too of the role of neurodiversity, opening new possibilities for people who might otherwise be stigmatised for being 'on the autism spectrum.'

And yet...

Many of us find it easier NOT to deal with difference and indeed find it threatening. Familiarity equals comfort, particularly for people operating from the conformist worldview. Left alone, many teams will gravitate towards consistency and homogeneity, as leaders knowingly or unknowingly recruit in their own image, and team members reinforce their own similarities rather than actively explore their differences.

TEAMS ARE POWERFUL VEHICLES FOR LEARNING
All too often, participants in individually focused initiatives, whether executive coaching or leadership development programmes, can struggle to implement new learning and behaviours in an unreceptive or uninformed team environment. Leadership itself is not simply a matter of individual behaviour – it is a relational activity that happens between a leader and other people. So, it makes sense to provide opportunities for leaders to develop and grow within their real-life context, working with their teams. When the development focus expands beyond the individual to the team, new possibilities emerge for sustaining and applying learning, through stronger peer relationships and shared accountability. As well as delivering on the organisational objectives, teams can become the engine room for learning and enhancing performance.

And yet...

Groupthink leads teams to succumb to a loss of independent thinking and an illusion of invulnerability. Rather than becoming a place of constructive challenge and learning, teams suffering from groupthink become a sinkhole of fearful conformity.

TEAMS CAN BE POWERFUL LEVERS OF STRATEGY AND CULTURE CHANGE

Trying to change a culture or lead on a new strategy as a single leader is inefficient. On the other hand, trying to influence a whole company at once using traditional channels becomes impractical. Teams are the sweet spot for change. In team conversations, leaders can help people to understand the real impact and relevance of new strategic initiatives in their working context. They can identify how to apply the changes in their work, and they can support each other to make these changes real.

Building connections *between* teams is also the fastest way of breaking down organisational siloes. When people experience a sense of true connection with others, and recognise their shared contributions to a common purpose, it becomes possible to reduce conflict and misunderstanding. Working at a team level makes it easier for people to develop a consistent set of performance habits that foster productive dialogue. This makes it easier for people to collaborate with and understand colleagues in different parts of the business.

And yet...

A team's norms (its unspoken rules of behaviour) are powerful and can be highly resistant to change. Rather than becoming a beacon of change, some teams can also 'hunker down' when threatened and become inward-looking and defensive. The feeling of 'us versus the world' (a classic group version of being below the line) reinforces this mindset and behaviour. It can be hard to help a team like this change. It will take patience and perhaps fresh leadership.

If organisations are going to make the most of teams, we all need to work with these paradoxes. Fortunately, that's what this chapter is all about!

Being an effective team member

We have already introduced the essential foundations that can help you become an effective and thriving team member. In Chapter 3, I described the importance of self-awareness as a pre-requisite for change and to help you manage your own emotional and motivational needs in a healthy manner. Now that we are talking teams, here is an added perspective; some psychologists say that your family of origin (the one you grew up in) was also your first team experience.[5] For many, your siblings were your first team-mates and your parent(s) your first leader(s). The ways of exerting influence, taking or avoiding responsibility, getting attention, fitting in or standing out that you developed in your first family, probably show up now when you are in a team. They are your survival patterns that you may rely on without you realising. They are especially likely to occur in times of stress or in a difficult relationship. Reflect on this possibility and see what you notice. Are you expecting your boss to behave like your parent? Are you treating a teammate like a younger sibling? Do you feel a sense of parental protection towards one of your team? These behaviours may, or may not, be helpful for you now. Just like we discussed in Chapter 3, becoming aware of these patterns with a sense of curiosity and self-compassion is the key to change.

In Chapter 5 I covered a range of relational skills that can help you to communicate and work with others. Clearly, you can apply these to your team experiences, but let me add a further consideration. As a team grows, the number of relationships increases exponentially. Think about it; a team of three people contains three different pairs. A team of five people contains ten pairs, while a team of ten people contains 45 pairs. An interacting team is only as strong as the weakest of its relationships, like links in a chain. So, you need to think about and attend to *all* your team relationships, ensuring that each one is at least 'good enough' to allow honest communication and feedback. This can take time, attention, and care, especially in a large team. Consider your relationships within your primary team – which ones are strong, which ones less so? What's the impact on you and your team's performance?

Finally, let's return to the worldviews we introduced in Chapter 2 and expand our understanding of these in relation to teams. Recall that at any given time, we understand and make sense of the world according to the worldviews we inhabit. Our access to new worldviews will often increase over time, and we are likely to have a 'centre of gravity' that defines us at any given point in our lives. Imagine what happens in a team where its members hold a range of worldviews – which of course is the case most of the time.

Otto Laske and Jan de Visch describe the dynamics of upward and downwardly divided teams.[6] A downwardly divided team is one in which the leader, or an influential team member, is operating from an earlier worldview than most of the team. If they hold enough power, they can 'drag' the team to operate at a lower level of complexity than they are capable of. This often shows up as a boss who is always diving into the detail, micromanaging, or failing to plan ahead. Conversely, an upwardly divided team has a leader or an influential team member who can work from a later worldview than most of the team. If this capacity is well-managed, it can lead to a team achieving higher levels of performance, greater foresight and better decision making. If you suspect either is happening in your team, look at the thought opening questions in Chapter 6. These are questions that increase the range of perspectives a team considers when tackling a problem. You may notice that versions of these are already present in an upwardly divided team – in which case dive in and lend your support – or are absent in a downwardly divided team. In this case, you might like to experiment with framing and inquiry (see again Chapter 3) using these types of questions.

A framework for exceptional teams

So far, I have described the strengths and challenges of working in teams and shown how you can apply healthy, high-performance principles to manage yourself and your working relationships. Let me now shift to the challenge of building and leading a thriving team. This section will be relevant if you are a team leader, or responsible for helping to support new or established teams.

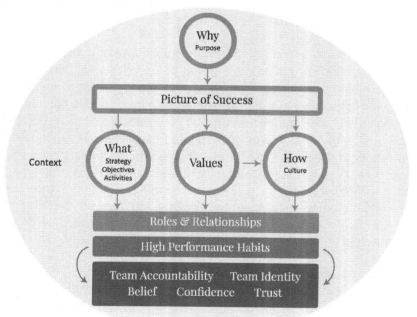

Figure 5 Mezzana Partners model of High Performing Teams

I spent several months working with my Mezzana Partners[7] colleagues to pool our knowledge and experience of working with teams over the last 30 years to develop the approach I am about to describe. We call this Exceptional Teams, and it brings together the elements of how you act, relate and think to illustrate the characteristics of a high performing team. This framework is adaptable and open enough to accommodate the wide variety of teams that exist in any modern business. You can use this to assess how well an established team is functioning and identify the high leverage areas of improvement. It also describes the sequence of four steps you go through to establish and develop a high performing team.

STEP 1: ESTABLISH A SHARED SENSE OF DIRECTION FOR THE TEAM.
As I will discuss in Chapter 8, one of the key roles of a leader is to establish a collective sense of purpose and direction that is shaped in response to your context. Ideally, a team's purpose will have a positive impact on the people, organisations, or environments in your context. Peter Hawkins, one of the pioneers of team coaching, describes this as the team's commission; the answer to the questions why are we here and who cares?[8] This may require you to look outside to the rest of your organisation, to your customers or clients, or to the wider world and consider how you will make a difference to those you serve.

Without a clear purpose you will at best be a collective of individuals with broadly aligned agendas; at worst, a group of individuals with conflicting objectives, plans and ways of working. Put starkly, if you cannot all articulate the same clear and compelling purpose then you are not a team. Having a clear purpose inspires motivation and gives meaning. It provides a sense of direction and energy. Your picture of success is a rich, vivid, shared description of what will be true if you successfully achieve your purpose. It helps your team members to understand what you are aiming for and how to know when you have arrived. Members of teams with a clear purpose and picture of success know how, and why, they are contributing to the company's strategy. They are clear too about who they serve, whether internal or external customers or stakeholders.

To clarify your team's purpose and contribution, you can apply the same approaches to motivation and alignment that we covered in Chapter 6. There are a couple of additional considerations to bear in mind. First, accept that delivering against your purpose may be a long game.

I worked closely with my Mezzana colleague John Anderson when he was Performance Director of British Canoeing's Olympic programme. In 1997 we began work to shape the purpose and ambition of the sport, and through a series of workshops with coaches, support staff and athletes we helped to define the World Class programme's purpose to be the number one nation in the Olympic disciplines. This felt quite a stretch at the time, as we had just returned from an unsuccessful campaign at the 1996 Atlanta Olympics. Yet, by holding steadfastly to this purpose the programme developed and by 2016 Great Britain was the most successful nation in Rio de Janeiro across slalom, sprint and paracanoe disciplines.

Anne's team

Remember Anne, the senior manager in a local authority responsible for children's social care? The pandemic was tough for Anne and her team. What was already a difficult job becoming impossible through the months of lockdown, and her department's caseload has skyrocketed. More children than ever need specialist support. Anne decides that she, and her team cannot go on. Supported by a team coach, Anne and her direct reports take a day off-site to patch up and catch up. The first hour or so is a bit rocky, the team aren't used to being all together in person, and it feels self-indulgent to be spending time and money like this when kids aren't being fed. But gradually the team relax and settle together and start to open up and share their stories and frustrations of the past year. Anne brings in the bigger picture of what's happening elsewhere in the local authority, and what she is learning from colleagues in other parts of the country. The team start to re-connect as humans not just job roles, and to build a new understanding of their shared context.

Sensing the time is right, the coach asks each person to share what first attracted them to social work. "I wanted to make a difference." "I had a crap childhood and did not want other kids to suffer like I did." "I liked that it was practical". The coach then invites the team to consider their purpose within this context. What is it that only they can do? Something profound and powerful has been unlocked within the team, the fatigue and cynicism overwhelmed by a deep connection with the team's purpose and contribution.

While talk of purpose and vision will be highly engaging for some, it may be a turn-off for those in your team who prefer to just 'get on with the job.' To them, it can all seem 'pie in the sky' or wishful thinking. Use their perspective to keep your work grounded and to identify the practical steps you will need to take if you are to achieve your long-term ambitions. There is nothing worse than a 'vision statement' gathering dust because the important work of translating it into action has been skipped. Which takes us nicely to the next step in building an Exceptional Team.

STEP 2: THE EXECUTION - YOUR WHAT AND HOW

Once you are aligned on WHY you exist and what you are aiming for, you need to understand what it takes to fulfil that purpose and achieve your picture of success. There are two parts to this – the first is WHAT you need to do – your strategy, tactics, and plans. Teams with aligned priorities tend to be successful (and cohesive). They have the discipline to stay focused on what's important and minimise being distracted by less important but apparently urgent demands. Each team member has clear personal objectives and the skills and resources they need to accomplish them. There is a logical flow between activities and outcomes, with a line of sight through to the team's – and whole company's – strategy and purpose. Again, use the Strategy Tree I described in Chapter 6 (see p90) to help your team to map out the connections between their activities and your purpose.

Anne's team

After a break for coffee and a walk outside, Anne and her team re-assemble. She begins the working session by laying out the department's key priorities for the next 12 months. Much of this is familiar to her team, but there are some surprises too, as over-worked team members realise what else is going on beyond their immediate role, and what has changed due to 'top down' decisions. Anne encourages the team to test and challenge her assumptions, and to share their ideas and best practice.

Guiding the team's task focus is your clear role as a leader, but leadership also requires attention to the team's culture, HOW its members need to 'be' as a team – what you believe, how you think and how you behave as a team. It is the 'soft' stuff that is so hard – your values and behaviours. Values must be more than a slogan, and they only have power when they are actively used to guide decisions. Do we take route A or route B? Do we invest here or there? Do we reward or sanction this behaviour? A company's values must underpin its choices, and by doing so its values start to shape and influence the company's collective behaviour and attitudes – its culture. Reinforcing your values and desired culture at a team level is a powerful way of changing the culture of a whole business. Peter Drucker is credited with saying "culture eats strategy for breakfast"[9] – meaning that no matter how clever the strategy, its successful execution relies on motivated, engaged, and creative employees.

As a leader, your values, behaviour, and mood cast a long shadow that will influence how your team members, think, act and relate, all of which shapes the level of psychological safety in your team. Harvard researcher Amy Edmondson defines psychological safety as– "a belief that one will not be punished or humiliated for speaking up with ideas, questions, concerns or mistakes.[10]" When teams have high levels of psychological safety, team members can challenge and be challenged skilfully, offering and receiving high levels of feedback. They can take risks, be more creative and more agile. Levels of delegation and openness can be higher. All of which means that learning is faster and more effective. When people are psychologically safe, they feel more comfortable to reveal themselves and bring more energy and authenticity to their role. Timothy Clark[11] usefully describes the following four stages of psychological safety and offers some practical tips on how to create it in a team:

Stage 1: Inclusion Safety
- Stay in contact and check in on people's needs and challenges
- Listen and pause before responding to input from your team
- Create opportunities to share experiences and bond
- Encourage people to connect with each other – especially new joiners

Stage 2: Learner Safety
- Share past mistakes
- Ask for help – demonstrate that it is ok 'not to know'
- Ask more questions than you offer solutions
- Show that you are learning too

Stage 3: Contributor Safety
- Ask people what they think
- Do not respond with anger, blame or shame to team-member's contributions
- Clarify how you make decisions
- Avoid shut down statements in meetings

Stage 4: Challenger Safety
- Invite constructive dissent
- When you reject feedback, say why
- Model vulnerability
- Weigh in last during a discussion
- Mandate a 'no interruption' rule in meetings

Anne's team

After the conversation on working priorities, which at times became heated as the team struggled to reconcile the gaps between their aspirations and their resources, the coach invites feedback on HOW they have just worked together. Each team member shares an observation about the process of the meeting – what they saw or heard happen: "I noticed that after I made a suggestion, Anne played it back so that everyone understood." "I noticed that I went quiet after Hannah interrupted me." The coach goes further, asking team members to say how they felt emotionally. "I felt affirmed," "I felt discouraged".

"So, how do you need to work together to bring out your best?" asks the coach. The team quickly collate a short list of the behaviours they aspire to using when they are together, along with an agreement to hold each other to account in future meetings.

STEP 3: ROLES AND RELATIONSHIPS

High performing teams do not just understand where they are headed and how to get there. They are also highly aware of their collective resources and strengths and how to best deploy them to fulfil their purpose. As I showed in Chapter 5, it is important that everyone is clear on their role; the contribution they bring to the team (expertise, knowledge, and qualities), and what they need from others in return. An effective team leader constantly assesses how the team is using its collective resource to meet the demand and achieve its goals; and can quickly identify when additional expertise may be required and move quickly to source that.

Pay attention to the patterns of communication and relationships in your team. Many teams still function as a "hub and spoke" with the leader as the hub, managing a series of bilateral relationships with each team member. If this is true for you, consider adding a rim to your wheel, to join up the working relationships between your team members. As a team leader explore your role in attending to all the key relationships in your team. Which are the strong and weak relationships? Which relationships would make the biggest positive difference if they were improved? You might want to introduce the Temperature Reading exercise from Chapter 5.

Team members in high performing teams seek to develop a high level of self-awareness, but this does not mean being self-centred. It means cultivating an understanding of their own behaviour and their impact on team-mates. It means being curious about others on the team and learning to value and appreciate differences. Rich and effective relationships are based on shared goals and clear roles, an understanding – and desire – to relate effectively with each other, and a genuine respect, caring and trust. Such relationships are not built overnight; team leaders understand the need to invest in relationships and spend time and energy to ensure there is a consistent high quality of relationships across the team.

Anne's team

The coach invites the team to reflect on their working relationships, and to identify which ones will be particularly important in coming months if they are to deliver their work plan. The team engage in a series of short meetings in pairs, to affirm and share feedback, their needs and appreciations of each other. Each person agrees with their colleague how to support each other in next phase of the team's work.

STEP 4: HIGH PERFORMANCE HABITS

Team leaders need to understand what makes an exceptional team. But everyone throughout the organisation needs a shared set of expectations about HOW they work in any team. This makes it easier for people to come together quickly and effectively, whether for a short-lived project team, when joining an established team, or even for a single meeting. There are four key high-performance habits, and when each person in a company both understands and is committed to applying them, then high performance teams will flourish:

1. Connection with purpose

There is always a risk that any team becomes too inward looking and self-protective – especially in times of stress and high workload. Indeed, this response of 'hunkering down' has helped human tribes survive over the eons! Yet in a modern organisation, team members need to look outward to connect with their purpose and stakeholders or clients. At the simplest level, team members need to be able to answer; 'why are we here?' and 'who do we serve?'. The answers to these simple questions can lead to a clear and compelling motivation and direction for the team. They apply just as much to an established team as to a group coming together to solve a specific problem. If team members cannot answer these questions, or they are not meaningful, then there is urgent work needed to clarify them, or perhaps it is time to disband!

2. Accountability

"Doing what you say you will do" may sound simple, and seemingly be easy to do. Yet lack of follow through is probably the biggest factor likely to derail a team. Teams easily drift into the domain of unfulfilled promises, incomplete actions, and the cycle of discussing the same topics and either not agreeing on actions or not following through on actions. In high performance teams, there is a shared and high commitment to following through on intentions. Members of a high performing team will ask for, and offer, support to get the job done for the greater good of the team. They have developed a language of accountability that is direct and honest, and this includes knowing when and how to say 'no' or 'not yet.' When a team member cannot meet a commitment, he or she raises it early and re-negotiates expectations. No more last-minute surprises about lack of delivery!

3. Balancing challenge and support

Leaders and members of high performing teams alike understand that high performance comes when challenge, direction and energy are balanced with mutual support and care for one another. Something magic happens when people fully realise that achieving high standards and treating people well are *not* mutually exclusive – in fact they are mutually supportive. This is summarised in the challenge and support matrix:

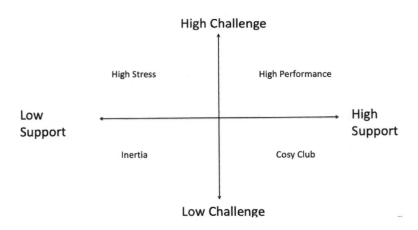

Figure 6 Challenge and Support Matrix

The personal mindset of 'staying above the line' (see Chapter 4) is essential to balance challenge and support because it creates the conditions for direct feedback and openness to learning. It also means that team members feel comfortable to express themselves without fear of attack or criticism. They feel like they can bring their real self to work, without having to compromise or limit their identity. These conditions of psychological safety enable high performance because team members are more willing to speak up, offer ideas and take risks. Creativity and energy are unlocked when people feel safe.

4. Always learning

High performing team members are hungry for feedback. Rather than being threatened by feedback, team members actively seek it out from each other and from their stakeholders. They are also direct and honest when they offer feedback because they know that it is essential for learning, and learning is essential for high performance. Whilst individuals hold an open and constructive attitude, the team itself will establish a rhythm of predict, prepare, perform, and review so that learning, and resilience, are embedded in its operations. These are the components of 'Thinking Straight' I described in Chapter 4.

Anne's team

The final part of the day involves the team reflecting on which of these high-performance habits are in place, and which need attention. They agree that over the next month they will focus on sustaining the balance of challenge and support that they experienced while being together in person. The coach will work with each of them online to build or strengthen this critical habit.

The outcomes – belief, confidence, and trust

Nearly every team leader I have ever worked with has asked for help to improve the level of trust in their team. These qualities are hard to create from scratch, and there are no silver bullets that will create trust, confidence and belief in a team. They do however emerge when a team is well aligned with the Exceptional Team framework, and they have discovered their unique team identity. John Syer, one of my early mentors, believed that a team's identity wasn't imposed from the outside.[12] It does not come from wearing the same t-shirt or baseball cap. He taught me that a team's identity is an immanent property that needs to be discovered and nurtured, by creating opportunities for team members to meet each other authentically and honestly. As a team's identity becomes clear, the sense of belonging and shared accountability increases. Trust is particularly reliant on the regular practice of accountability. After all, it is hard to trust team-mates if I do not believe they will do what they say they will do. But if I have direct and immediate evidence that my team-mates share a common purpose, have clear roles and responsibilities, and deliver on their commitments, then trust quickly builds.

Anne's team

After an intense day that seemed to pass in just moments, Anne's team leave feeling empowered and refreshed. Each has greater clarity about the why, what, and how of their work together. They commit to another day offsite in 4 months.

The Five Cs

Five factors are necessary to create a healthy, motivated team culture. People and performance will thrive if you can create these conditions in your team, because they align to the basic human needs that we've been discussing through this book. Reflect on how you feel personally and regularly take stock with team members to identify any areas that need attention:

Remote and hybrid teams

The COVID pandemic has accelerated organisational change like no other event in recent times. Companies were forced to adapt fast to remote and home working, and we all came to love or loath screen-based interactions, with "you are on mute" replacing "who wants a coffee?" as the most-used phrase in team meetings. People vary greatly in their response to remote working based on personality and circumstance. Introverts love it, extroverts hate it. Those with a spare room or home office can thrive in ways that are impossible when juggling a laptop perched on the edge of your bed. There has been a loss of connection and free exchange, those water cooler conversations that kept people in the loop. It is hard to build new relationships and more difficult to train and induct new starters into your company culture. Yet many organizations report higher productivity, whilst costs have been reduced. Individuals report the benefits of increased flexibility and autonomy to manage their lives at home, whilst avoiding the trudge and cost of a regular commute.

Hybrid working, where teams spend some time in the office and some time at home looks likely to be the norm in the future. It has proved more effective, and more popular with employees, than anyone expected. However, the tribal sense of belonging that is one of the key benefits of a team, has been compromised.

This has shown itself in two ways.

1. RESOLVING CONFLICT
Remote working makes it harder to overcome conflict, because it is so much easier to misconstrue email or text messages compared to speaking, and screen-based communication can give the illusion of real contact without any of the subtleties of whole-body language. This is where face-to-face contact matters; it is an essential opportunity to reconnect at a human level and re-affirm that while the other person may have a different perspective, fundamentally we are working together on the same thing.

2. STRETCHED BOUNDARIES, STRESSED PEOPLE
Hybrid working has created expectations of faster response times, and the challenge to maintain effective boundaries between 'home time', switched off from work, and 'work time' where you can fully focus away from domestic demands. This blurring has increased the load and stress levels, especially for those with domestic or childcare responsibilities. This comes at a time of greater worries about personal health, reduced freedom of

movement and the overarching uncertainties of climate and unstable geopolitics. We are all impacted by increased background stress that decreases our psychological flexibility to engage productively with conflict and difference.

What does this mean for teams? Single and smaller teams are often working as well if not better in hybrid form, but larger teams and sub-teams are often struggling to maintain the level of psychological safety and trust that continues to build high performance. Similarly, in teams needing to work with other teams across the organization, this capability has been eroded, and relationships can be more fragile.

WHAT CAN YOU DO IF YOU ARE LEADING A HYBRID TEAM?
In addition to all the principles I have described so far to build and lead an Exceptional team, you can also:

- Create short term clarity. It can be hard to be confident about the long-term future so focus more on the short-term certainty – map out the stepping stones that will take the team forward.
- Use the 5 Cs to tune into your individual team member's motivation and wellbeing. Remember that we are all responding differently to the challenges and opportunities of hybrid working, and do not assume that your team all have the same needs. Remember too that your team member's personal situation can change (a new child arriving, splitting up from a partner, moving house) and this may have a significant impact on their capacity to manage hybrid working.
- Use a range of communication channels. Although we have all moved to Zoom and Teams, old school phone calls still work and can make it easier to get away from the desk to 'walk and talk'.
- Take a thoughtful approach to how you use time together in the office. Asking your team to come into the office and then having them spend the whole day on video calls is a poor use of time and energy. Use time in the office to do the things you cannot do productively online. Creative work, problem solving, coaching and team development all work better face to face. Think of going to the office as the new off-site meeting.
- Keep exploring and experimenting. Hybrid work is new for nearly everyone, so stay proactive to keep learning about what works for you and your team.

Conclusion

Whatever changes the future holds, one thing is certain; we will continue to work in teams. And teams will continue to hold the key to the quality of lived experience at work and to the creativity and productivity that we all rely on to thrive. It is up to each of us to take responsibility to be at our best, both as a team member and a team leader.

Want to work on this?

Here are a series of High-Performance Team Habits for team leaders. Choose one to work on and share this with your team. This has several benefits. It increases accountability especially if you ask for feedback on your progress, and it shows that you are taking your own growth seriously.

- When I communicate with my team, instead of focusing just on tasks and tactics, I will ensure everyone is aligned with our purpose and picture of success.
- When I start my working day, instead of assuming my team members are all operating normally, I will check in with how they are feeling.
- When I have finished meeting with a team member, instead of taking their ongoing development for granted, I will identify one small, specific learning area to focus on the next time we meet.

Want to know more?

Psychological safety is an important underpinning for team performance. I've touched on it this chapter and if you want to go deeper, I recommend looking at the work of Amy Edmondson. She coined the phrase and has written and spoken extensively about it.

Here is a useful starting point to her work:
https://www.hbs.edu/faculty/Pages/profile.aspx?facId=6451 (accessed 09-03-2023)

Also see Tim Clark's (2020) book *The 4 stages of psychological safety; defining the path to inclusion and innovation.* Berrett-Koehler Publishers.

---

[1] Sinek quoted on *https://www.linkedin.com/posts/simonsinek_a-team-is-not-a-group-of-people-who-work-activity-6780192942679179264-pYtP/*
[2] For example, see What is Total Quality Management (TQM)? *https://asq.org/quality-resources/total-quality-management*
[3] Katzenbach, R. & Smith, D. K. (1993)

[4] For more on of how diversity improves teams, see the McKinsey Report *Diversity Wins,* from 2020, available at
https://www.mckinsey.com/featured-insights/diversity-and-inclusion/diversity-wins-how-inclusion-matters

[5] Syer, J. & Connolly, C. (1996)

[6] De Visch, J. & Laske, O. (2020)

[7] For more on our company and how we work, see *www.mezzanapartners.com*

[8] Hawkins, P. (2011).

[9] Yet he may never have said it at all – see:
https://quoteinvestigator.com/2017/05/23/culture-eats/

[10] Edmonson, A. (2023).

[11] Clark, T. (2023)

[12] Syer, J. (1986)

Chapter 8. Leading in new worlds

Now we explore how you can use your capacities to think, relate and act to lead others and enable them to thrive in a healthy high performing workplace. We will begin by considering the nature of the post-modern world – especially given the massive upheaval created by the 2020 COVID-19 pandemic. I believe that this has accelerated and made visible existing leadership challenges, and that we were already living and working in a volatile, fast changing world. Then, we will look at what leadership means in this complex context and explore why the way we usually think about leadership needs to evolve, fast. Rather than seeing leaders as individual heroes, we need to start thinking of leaders as coaches and explorers, hearth holders and agitators, all working together in service of a shared purpose. These roles will be essential as we start to re-imagine the world of work for the coming decade.

Summary

- We need new mental maps to make sense of a complex world.
- A complex world also means we need to re-imagine the meaning of leadership.
- Leadership can no longer rely only on heroic individuals.
- Instead, we need to develop the collective capacity for leadership.
- Four leadership archetypes are essential: hearth holders and agitators, coaches and explorers.
- Accessing these archetypes in a healthy manner requires an inner readiness.
- The future won't be any easier than the present, and we have a responsibility to prepare for it now.

What sort of world are we living in?

Even before the COVID pandemic, many of us were living in an increasingly complex context. In these conditions, leaders were asking their people to be more agile, more collaborative, more outcome-focused, and more innovative. The 2020s were already presenting us with big, complex and inter-connected challenges over the coming decade. These include:

If you do business in or with the UK, then adapting to a post-Brexit world is going to take up a lot of your attention.

As I write this, the full impact of Brexit on the UK's trading and social relationship is still being realised.[1] Many businesses have suffered from increased costs, paperwork and friction in terms of exporting or importing, leading some businesses to close or move offshore. Coupled with the Ukraine war we find ourselves in a time of crisis as supply chains are disrupted and costs skyrocket.

Responding to the climate emergency and its impacts on consumer behaviour, supply chains and resources, employee well-being, travel and even your social license to trade.

It feels like awareness of the climate emergency, brought about by a combination of poor land and water management, over-population, deforestation, and carbon emissions, has finally broken into the public consciousness. The COVID pandemic has reinforced the danger of deforestation as a major factor in the spread of zoonotic diseases. No business is immune from increasing disruption, whether it is caused by extreme weather events preventing employees or customers reaching you, a change in buying habits as consumers start to shun certain products (for example cheap 'disposable' fashion), government regulation banning single use plastic,[2] or investors putting pressure on banks to divest from fossil fuel-based companies.[3] I predict that companies that fail to respond or re-position in relation to the climate emergency are going to become pariahs – both to customers and investors.

Staying meaningful for your employees and profitable as a business in the face of rapid technological, political, and social change.

One CEO in the commercial property world recently said to me "we have seen more change in our industry over the last two years than in the previous thirty." Like many sectors, his business is facing competition from game changing entities that did not exist a few years ago. But it is turbulent, so a company like WeWork went from being an existential threat to established property managers to almost a laughingstock within months.[4] Technology and Artificial Intelligence means that much of the transactional work can be done faster and cheaper, and with far fewer people. 'Old hands' who relied on personal relationships and closing deals over a serious lunch are now struggling for a meaningful role. Retaining the engagement of your people, and staying profitable as a business, have never been harder.

The COVID pandemic has accelerated this volatile, complex and uncertain context. Rather than more change in two years than the last thirty, in 2020 we saw more change in three months than the last thirty. Companies were forced to fast track technological and social changes in a matter of weeks; homeworking, video meetings and reduced business travel are now the new normal. Those companies that fail to re-invent themselves for this new reality face extinction and believing that we will 'return to normal' is either ignorance or avoidance. The pandemic has also made visible what was already there. Just like adding stain to a microscope slide reveals the details of a cell, COVID revealed the social and economic patterns within which we were living: the risks of 'just in time' supply chains, the interconnectedness of world trade and travel, the inequalities between those engaged in knowledge work and 'unskilled' care workers on zero hours contracts.

Although few business leaders have ever faced a situation as overwhelming, unpredictable, and serious as the COVID pandemic, the principles for navigating these challenges are well understood, if not widely known. One of the most useful guides is the Cynefin (the Welsh word for habitat) framework, developed by David Snowden and Mary Boone.[5] It helps leaders assess their specific context and choose appropriate leadership strategies as conditions vary and change.

Cynefin – a map for new worlds

Snowden and Boone use Cynefin to describe five different contexts, simple, complicated, complex, chaotic and disordered:

Simple and complicated contexts assume an ordered universe, where cause-and-effect relationships are perceptible, and right answers can be determined based on the facts and by drawing on experience. Simple domains rely on routines, the application of best practice and standard operating procedures. This is a predictable and known world. Complicated domains rely on specialised expertise and knowledge. The right answer may not be obvious but assembling the right experts and applying rigorous analysis will reveal it.

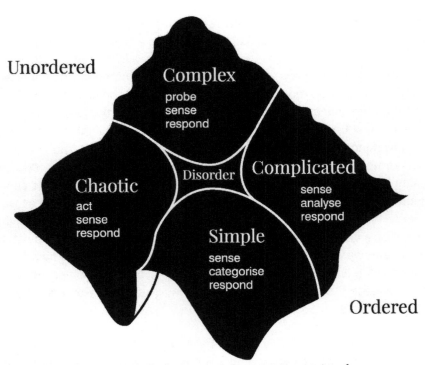

Figure 7 Cynefin - A Leader's Framework for Decision Making[6]

In these contexts, it makes sense to think of organisations as machines – logical, efficient, linear and with clear inputs and outputs. A car's engine is indeed a good metaphor. When I first started driving in the late 70s, cars were simple and many people did their own basic maintenance, changing the oil, putting in new spark plugs, and tinkering with the carburettor timing. I even had friends who would take it much further, happily stripping down and even replacing the whole engine on their front drive. Forty years on, and cars have gone from mostly simple to complicated. Opening the bonnet reveals a bewildering combination of sealed black boxes that I barely recognise as an engine. Maintaining and repairing a modern car requires specialised electronic diagnostics, tools and expertise beyond the reach of the average driver. But even if I can no longer make much sense of a modern engine, there are experts who can, and I can rely on them (generally!) to identify and fix a problem.

The key difference between a complicated and complex context is the nature of the relationships within each one. To draw on my friend Alistair Mant's work in this area, it is like the difference between a frog and a bicycle.[7] Both frogs and bicycles can be thought of as systems – in that they have constituent parts that interact with each other. A bicycle, however, lives in the ordered world of the simple and complicated. Why? Because with the right tools, a mechanic can strip a bike down to its component parts, replace or upgrade any of these parts, and re-build the whole thing to end up with a better bike. The different components of a bike interact, but they are not inter-dependent.

By contrast, even the most skilled veterinary surgeon cannot strip a frog down to its component parts, then re-assemble a better frog. At an early stage of disassembly, the frog will stop being a frog, despite its parts all being together on the operating table. The different components of a frog interact, and critically, are also interdependent on each other. The elements cannot function in isolation; they rely on and influence other components of the system. Together they create what we see as a frog, but this 'frogginess' is an emergent property that is greater than the sum of the parts. A bike is the sum of its parts, but no more. If I leave my bike in the shed for a year, I can dust it off, oil the chain and it will be as good as the bike I had before. Depending on when I encounter the frog, it might be spawn, a tadpole, or a frog.

All complex systems and contexts share this key feature of interdependence. This means that we do not always recognise or understand the relationship between cause and effect. There are many interacting elements, and even a small change in one will have impacts on many other parts, which in turn will respond and impact others in an interconnected web of relationships. Complex contexts are products of their history, but this does not mean we can use the past to predict the future. They are subject to sudden, unexpected shifts that may have no precedent. With hindsight we may be able to understand these radical changes, but we cannot foresee them. Imagine if you had been standing in a 'wet meat' market in the Chinese city of Wuhan in late 2019. As you watched traders sell bat meat could you have forecast how the COVID pandemic would unfold?

Rather than a mechanistic world view, we need to think of complex contexts using different metaphors – as living systems rather than machines. A beautiful example of the move from complicated to complex leadership comes from the work of Isabella Tree and Charlie Burrell, described in her book *Wilding*.[8] This is the story of how they gave up trying to make a living from their Sussex farm using a complicated mindset – striving for efficiency, trying to drive up crop yields, investing in more and more expensive machinery, and instead recognised that they were dealing with a complex natural phenomenon. Their part of Sussex had heavy clay soil which meant that no matter how much fertilizer they applied, or how big a combine harvester they used, it was never going to be a 'competitive' place for modern agriculture. By learning to work with their property holistically, over the years it has developed into one of Europe's most important habitats for a wide range of endangered species and attracts world-wide interest.

Leaders need different mindsets and skills to lead in complex contexts; the ability to engage in dialogue, to establish safe experiments, and to look for patterns. We will discuss these more shortly. First, let's cover the remaining two contexts described by Cynefin, chaotic and disordered.

The first few weeks of the COVID pandemic had all the features of an un-ordered, chaotic context. It was fast changing and turbulent, and in this highly uncertain period many people felt high levels of tension, anxiety and even fear. There were many unknowns, and there was a need for fast and decisive action without the luxury of having all available information. Having 'best practice' to hand proved to be of limited value, especially if it was politically inconvenient. We are now learning that much of the UK government's pandemic response was based on the assumptions relevant to influenza, which has different characteristics to a coronavirus. By assuming that past learning and best practice would be adequate, the government severely misread a complex problem.[9]

A *disordered* context is particularly challenging. Depending on where and how you look, you may see some or all, of the other four contexts in play. No single one is prominent. It can be difficult to make sense, and it might be necessary to adopt parallel approaches simultaneously. A war zone or the immediate period after an earthquake or other natural disaster are examples of a disordered context.

Given the VUCA world in which we live, what does leadership mean and what do leaders need to do?

Regardless of what your world looked like pre-COVID, leaders now need to recognise that the rules have changed. The coming decade will predominantly be a time of complex problems, in uncharted territory with few tried and tested solutions. This requires leaders to develop new capabilities, one of the most important is to navigate polarities – "two interdependent and seemingly contradictory states that must be maintained for success over time."[10] We encounter many polarities in organisational life; do we centralise or decentralise? Diversify or specialise? Develop individuals or build teams? The nature of a polarity means that both poles are valuable and necessary, just like a tightrope needs to be secure at both ends. Each end is interdependent – you cannot have one without the other. Polarities can be tricky to manage because our brains are wired to prefer clear-cut, either-or choices. And in many situations an either – or choice is fine; if the building is burning down, I would much prefer a clear choice to leave than to stay! But binary, either/or thinking is not helpful when working with a polarity, because both dimensions offer value, and both sides become problematic when overused.

Whilst there are many polarities, there are three that are particularly relevant for leaders in the coming decade because they are universal to any business or sector. They are also the most salient when it comes to creating a healthy high performing workplace.

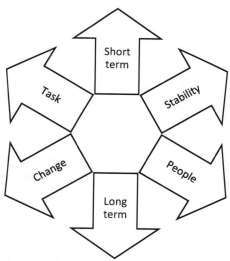

As a leader, you probably feel most comfortable working at one end or the other of each of these dimensions. But in a complex world it is no longer possible (if it ever was) to privilege one or the other of these poles. Within each polarity, both poles are essential and just like the component parts of a frog, all six are interdependent. We must learn to work with them systemically rather than in isolation. To do so, we must challenge the very notion of what makes a leader. We need to re-examine the deeply ingrained models of leadership we have absorbed through popular culture, the media, and even our own experience.

We don't need another hero

Take a moment and think of your favourite leader, the person you hold as your role model. If you struggle to think of a real person, what about a leader from films, books and myths? Over the years I have asked many people to do this and share their examples. Often, people describe famous politicians like Winston Churchill or Nelson Mandela. Or business leaders like Richard Branson or Bill Gates. Often men, these examples reinforce the idea that leadership comes down to the courage and insight of one key individual who single-handedly turns around the fortunes of his people in the face of adversity. This is often called 'heroic leadership.'

While the role of individual leaders is, and always will be, important, I question the relevance of heroic leadership in today's businesses.[11] It places unrealistic expectations on leaders and their followers – even though deep down we know that all heroes have 'feet of clay' it is always a disappointment to discover this for ourselves. Pragmatically, making sense of a VUCA environment is too much for any one person. Different skill sets and experiences need to be brought to bear on complex issues and managing the three polarities I have just described needs more than one brain. Heroic leadership places too much influence in the hands of a single individual and ignores the inter-connectivity and competing needs of today's complex world. Also, the accompanying metaphor of business as warfare (vanquishing the virus, defeating your competitors, winning new markets, defending your territory) is inadequate for the challenges we face in the coming decade because it leads to a short term, win/lose mentality that limits more creative and collaborative thinking. In a complex world, today's business leaders are not standing alone against a single, well-defined enemy that can be overcome by a cavalry charge or an inspiring speech.

The heroic leader is an example of an archetype. An archetype is a character or story that transcends time and culture. They have their origins in our oldest myths, stretching back many thousands of years. Archetypes resonate deeply within us because they speak to the essence of being human.

Popular culture has long drawn on archetypes. Successful books, films and TV shows often feature archetypal plots and characters; for example, have you noticed that Star Wars and the Lord of the Rings are essentially the same story?[12] Reluctant heroes like Bilbo Baggins/Luke Skywalker must go on a quest accompanied by brave companions (Hans Solo/Aragorn), guided by a wise elder (Gandalf/Obi Ben Kenobi) and battle against evil (Darth Vader/ Sauron). So, as we go through our lives we are exposed to a wide array of archetypal heroes, villains, warriors and damsels in distress. These ancient archetypes and contemporary cultural stereotypes will shape the way we think, act and respond as leaders.

New archetypes for leadership — hearth holders and agitators, coaches and explorers

How then might we think of leadership if we want to let go of individually based heroic leadership? Hearth holders, agitators, coaches and explorers are four different archetypes that can equip leaders to thrive in complexity. Each archetype holds a particular focus on the dimensions of people and task, stability and change. All four are relevant in the short term, focusing on immediate priorities, and in taking a long-term view toward the future. As you read about each one, mentally 'try it on for size' and notice which feel comfortable for you, and which feel unfamiliar. We can each tap into all these archetypes — because archetypes are universal — but that does not mean all these characteristics should be embodied, all the time, in a single individual. That would just take us back to the (super) hero template! Notice which ones you can access most readily, and which ones you might explore and perhaps 'grow into.' Think too about your close colleagues and which archetypes they do, or could, embody. It is important to think about how these archetypes can be combined within a leadership team, because it is only through shared dialogue and mutual inquiry that leaders can effectively make sense of complexity.

Before describing each of these archetypes in detail, there are two further considerations: your inner readiness, and awareness of the shadow.

Your inner readiness to lead

While I want to downplay the idea of the solitary heroic leader, this does not mean your individual qualities and development are unimportant. To embody fully and maturely any of these leadership archetypes requires you to develop your internal readiness to lead. Sadly, there are many examples where people have sought out, or been placed in, leadership roles without being ready, and the results are not pretty. If you have ever encountered a leader who is a bully, refuses to admit they are wrong, is a control freak, or chronically avoids tough decisions, then you have experienced the consequences of a lack of inner readiness. As author Douglas Adams said:

"It is a well-known fact that those people who most want to rule people are, ipso facto, those least suited to do it... anyone who is capable of getting themselves made President should on no account be allowed to do the job."[13]

DEVELOPING YOUR READINESS TO LEAD

Developing your readiness to lead requires humility, a willingness to learn and to admit when you have got it wrong. The world we live in is complex and changing so fast that it is impossible for any one person to hold enough knowledge and experience within their own heads to make sense of it all. This is especially true for those in leadership roles. Those who seek only to assert and defend their own point of view may be right some of the time (as the proverb says, even a broken clock is right twice a day) but they cannot expect to bring people with them on the journey. Mature leaders ask questions, are open to feedback, and can listen to alternative opinions without feeling threatened. They are constantly striving to know themselves better and to learn.

Inner readiness does not mean reaching perfection as a human being. None of us ever have, and none of us ever will, achieve perfection. Every leader has 'feet of clay' because every leader is a human being. Indeed, it is deeply unhelpful to expect or demand otherwise of ourselves or others. But to lead in a way that seeks to provide a thriving, purposeful workplace, we must be willing to acknowledge our own humanity and constantly grow our self-awareness.

Within each of the archetypes we are about to explore, there are very specific requirements for inner readiness. Each requires us to grow beyond a natural comfort zone into what feels like its opposite. You will recall we explored these changes earlier in Chapter 3 when we looked at how the motives and drives that get us to a certain point in our career won't take us further.

Look out for the shadow

A key aspect of mythology, brought into modern awareness by Carl Jung, is the idea of the shadow.[14] This is the hidden opposite of any archetype, necessary for its existence but often problematic when first encountered. Consider the characters in Star Wars – and the way Darth Vader (the dark father) tempts Luke Skywalker over to the dark shadow side of power. Less dramatically, any human quality becomes a weakness when it is overplayed; persistence turns to stubbornness, caution becomes risk aversion, creativity leads to chaos. Without inner readiness, you are more likely to succumb to the shadow side of each of the archetypes, so I point them out to help you stay aware of their presence.

People and task: coach and explorer

Many businesses succeeded through the twentieth century by applying the principles of Taylorism; standardising tasks into a rigid, yet efficient production line. People became 'human resources' to be managed with the same rational objectivity as any other raw material, their roles tightly defined, and performance closely monitored. People were necessary for achieving the organisation's task but had no inherent value. For at least the last 30 years critics have argued that this mechanistic approach has run its course, yet many of its tenets still hold sway.[15] The fact is, this approach works, at least in simple, and some complicated contexts. In a complex world, we need a different approach.

We encountered 'Deliberately Developmental Organisations' earlier in Chapter 2. These "operate on the foundational assumptions that adults can grow; that not only is attention to the bottom line and the personal growth of all employees desirable, but the two are interdependent; that both profitability and individual development rely on structures that are built into every aspect of how the company operates; and that people grow through the proper combination of challenge and support, which includes recognizing and transcending their blind spots, limitations, and internal resistance to change"[16]. This definition offers a third way of managing the people and task polarity to succeed in a complex world. Leaders need to think differently about the relationship between people and the work they do. Two archetypes make this possible; the Coach who helps people to grow and learn, and the Explorer who provides drive, energy, and vision.

COACH: ENABLING PEOPLE TO GROW, LEARN AND PERFORM
Since the late 1980s we have seen the emergence of professional executive coaches whose role is to support leaders to learn and perform better. Yet this modern role draws on a much older and universal archetype.

Some years ago, I was on a white-water kayaking trip on the White Nile in Uganda. For the first two days we hired a local guide, Manut. He spoke English well, and unusually for people in his village, had travelled to Europe when he competed in a kayaking championship. As we paddled across a wide lake towards the rapids, we started to talk. He was curious – "what do you do for a job?" he asked. I explained my role as an executive coach working with senior leaders, helping them reflect, learn, and improve their performance in tough jobs. Manut paused for a few moments, then said "so you are like an uncle." He explained that in his culture, it was the uncle's role to provide perspective and guidance to talk over problems, with a sense of caring and distance that a father might struggle to provide.

Whether a symbolic uncle or aunt, a leader who embodies the coach archetype champions the learning, growth, and wellbeing of people, doing so directly with individuals as a coach or mentor, or by ensuring the organisation's culture and processes align learning with performance. Peter Senge said it best back in 1990–"the only sustainable competitive advantage is an organization's ability to learn faster than the competition."[17] More than thirty years later, in the complex and fast changing world we live in, this statement rings truer than ever. We need leaders who can help their people learn and adapt, fast. Leaders who can help their people sustain wellbeing and motivation, and to maintain connection with each other in a virtual environment.

The inner readiness to embody the coach archetype is to switch from gaining your primary satisfaction from your own achievement, to enjoying the process of enabling others to achieve. We discussed a version of this dynamic back in Chapter 5 in relation to moving from a self to other focus when managing healthy relationships. Making this psychological switch from self to other does NOT mean becoming some sort of altruistic saint – or even worse a self-sacrificing martyr! A mature response involves learning to navigate between an appropriate and healthy self-regard, and the ability to 'de-centre' and put the needs of others first. I have seen this shift most vividly when a sportsperson retires and moves to a coaching role. Most struggle initially to make the psychological switch from being self-centred, almost a pre-requisite for an elite athlete, to being other-centred, essential for a coach or leader. Regardless of technical ability, those who cannot make this inner change rarely become great coaches.

The coach's shadow lies in over-emphasising human needs to the detriment of all else, creating an overly 'cosy' culture in which people avoid holding others to account for fear of conflict. It can also lead to avoiding or fudging decisions that are right for the whole business but have a negative impact on some employees. For example, delaying a necessary organisational change because it will lead to job losses. This risk is offset by the Explorer's energy and drive – which we turn to now.

EXPLORER: INSPIRING AND GUIDING ACTION TOWARDS THE ORGANIZATION'S PURPOSE

I recently watched the animated Disney movie Moana and discovered why it is a favourite for my daughters. The lead character epitomises the Explorer archetype, venturing out beyond the safety of her home island on a mission to save her people. She battles with her conservative father and helps him overcome his fear of the unknown to succeed, and (spoiler alert) she eventually leads her people on an inspiring voyage to safety.

Like Moana, leaders also need to think and behave as if they are explorers guiding an expedition across uncharted territory. Along the journey the whole group needs to stay together, so there is no advantage to charging off alone or leaving people behind. The leader's role is to assess the environment and discern which way to go, to keep the group connected and engaged, and to draw on the diverse talents of the group to overcome the emerging challenges they face together. Success comes by adapting to a challenging landscape and maintaining movement (and indeed survival) together.

Driven by a deep purpose, explorers provide the energy and motivation that inspires others to follow, even when the destination is unknown and success far from certain. As in the (apocryphal) 1900 advertisement for a polar expedition: "Men wanted for hazardous journey to the South Pole. Small wages, bitter cold, long months of complete darkness, constant danger. Safe return doubtful. Honour and recognition in case of success."[18] Explorers know that there are few long-term certainties in a complex world, and that direction is more important than destination. By enabling, guiding, cajoling, and engaging, the explorer is the catalyst for directed movement.

A willingness to journey into the unknown should not imply an absence of fear. I know from my experience as a whitewater kayaker that the most dangerous people to venture with are the ones without fear. They are more likely to take ill-considered risks that endanger everyone. Fear, and its close cousin anxiety, are useful guides but poor masters. To access the explorer archetype with maturity, leaders must learn how to manage, but not ignore, their own fear and anxiety. In particular, to resist reacting to the anxiety that is generated by uncertainty and ambiguity. It is often essential to hold options open, or to choose without full information. In both cases, poor decisions are often based on the need to resolve the discomfort of not knowing.

The explorer's shadow side is to become so obsessed by the success of the mission that people are mistreated or left behind. The ends begin to justify the means, and the wellbeing and growth of people are sacrificed by a myopic focus on the end result. Ideally this risk is offset by a strong coach, who can help the explorer to remain self-aware and maintain a big picture view of the enterprise.

Stability and change: hearth holder and agitator

In the face of accelerating change and unpredictability, 'agile' has emerged as a new approach to teams and organisations over recent years. IT consultancy Gartner call agile a 'bi-modal' approach, one that maintains a stable backbone of support functions and specialist capabilities to capture learning and provide efficiency, with fluid teams that come together quickly to pursue opportunities and develop new products that co-create value for customers.[19] Like Deliberately Developmental Organisations, Agile is an attempt to find a 'both - and' approach to stability and change. Creating and leading agile organisations is difficult because different, yet complementary, leadership skills are needed. These skills and differences are embodied by the archetypes of the Hearth holder maintaining stability and the Agitator driving change.

HEARTH HOLDER: TAKING CARE OF PRACTICALITIES AND MAKING WISE USE OF RESOURCES
In many tribal cultures, one of the most important roles was the guardian of the fire.[20] This person was responsible for keeping fire alive, even carrying carefully wrapped embers from place to place as the tribe travelled. Whilst others would venture out to hunt and gather food, this tribe member stayed in the camp and ensured that their fire, critical for their

survival, hard to start, and easy to extinguish, kept burning. The hearth holder archetype draws on this ancient tradition. Serving the needs of others before their own, the hearth holder safeguards the wellbeing of people, processes, and resources.

Sir David Attenborough embodies this archetype in our current culture. By calling attention to the natural world – the source of all our resources – he invites us all to act now in service of our long-term survival.

The role of a company director to look after shareholder's assets, also draws on this archetype. Sadly, this aspect of the company director's role has been overlooked for many years in favour of simply delivering the greatest profit. Increasingly, there is a recognition that this role needs to extend beyond a company's tangible goods and finances to include all its stakeholders; staff, customers, suppliers and even society and the broader environment. In the 2020s, hearth holders must care about and attend to the triple bottom line of profit, people, and planet.[21] They think long term, or as Simon Sinek calls it, they play the infinite game.[22] Mature hearth holding is not a finite game of defeating the opposition or winning market share, but about enabling your people to learn and thrive through the pursuit of meaningful work alongside people they respect and care about.

The inner readiness to fully embody the hearth holder and go from simply managing the bottom line, requires a move from narrow self-interest to caring for others and the environment. Those who can only take a self-serving view will struggle to encompass and appreciate all the stakeholders that contribute to a business's success. The shadow side of the hearth holder is to become too risk averse and unwilling to change. Caring and conserving does not mean resisting all change, and indeed it is increasingly necessary to embrace change if we are to preserve things we value – like fresh air and water. Excessive risk aversion in heart holders may well be triggered by an unruly Agitator, and we will learn more about this archetype now.

AGITATOR: CHALLENGING CONVENTION AND INNOVATING NEW WAYS OF WORKING

Agitators are impatient with the status quo and seek to create and innovate new and better ways of working. Think of Steve Jobs who relentlessly pushed Apple to refine its products and technology, entrepreneurs like Richard Dyson who challenged conventional wisdom, or activists like Greta

Thunberg who speak truth to power. Agitators are not always easy to live or work with, and their constant challenge and impatience can easily rub people the wrong way. Yet to thrive in a complex world we need leaders who are willing to experiment, take risks, and challenge convention. They drive invention and change.

Sometimes this shows up as a "healthy disregard" for authority, a willingness to turn a blind eye when rules are broken in pursuit of innovation. Or in a relentless intellectual curiosity, that questions the old way of doing things and seeks to break with the past. Agitators support their team to question their own values and expectations, as well as those of their organisation. Team members are also encouraged to think on their own, address challenges, and develop creative solutions. Agitators get others to look at problems from different angles.

The inner work for agitators is to overcome a fear of rejection or ridicule. If a leader's self-esteem relies on acceptance by others, then it is difficult, if not impossible, to innovate or speak truth to power. Mature agitators no longer rely on being accepted by the group and have learned to voice their ideas without being held back by a need for approval. Author and philosopher Ayn Rand took this archetype to an extreme in her novel *The Fountainhead*, the story of architect Howard Roark who would rather see his magnificent building destroyed than his vision compromised. Roark reveals the shadow side of the Agitator, who has become incapable of working within boundaries or aligning to a shared vision.[23] There needs to be a healthy respect between Hearth holders and Agitators, with both recognising the complementary value they each bring.

The relationship between the archetypes

We have said that in a complex world, leadership cannot rely on a charismatic individual rousing the troops by giving a grand speech. We have also recognised that leaders need to navigate several key polarities. But how do the four archetypes work together? The answer lies in understanding the relationships – and tensions – within and between the Hearth Holder, Agitator, Coach and Explorer. Within a leadership team it is likely that different members will gravitate toward a particular archetype based on their natural styles and skills. A team member may also hold an archetype for a specific situation – say advocating change in relation to how a task is carried out.

Two key factors influence how well a team can use the archetypes: identity and relationships.

IDENTITY

It is easy to become over-invested in any of the archetypes. I may come to value the capacity to agitate so much that it becomes 'who I am' not 'what I do.' This is most likely to occur for people working from an expert worldview (see Chapter 2) but anyone can be 'had by' their professional identity and values, as we saw when we explored self-awareness in Chapter 3. When a team member is 'had by' an archetype he or she is far more likely to overuse its strengths and fall into its shadow expression. It becomes much harder to both notice your own over-use and to acknowledge the benefits of the opposing view on the other side of the polarity. Rather than creatively seeking a 'third way' that brings the best of both sides, competing positions seesaw back and forth in conflict and acrimony.

RELATIONSHIPS

When each person has done enough of the inner work to be ready to access and hold an archetype, it is possible to develop relationships based on mutual respect, rather than use energy defending your own identity and values. A team can hold and then start to creatively explore the polarities they face through creative dialogue.

These dynamics can also show up internally, as tensions between the different internal selves that make up your professional identity. Feeling like you are both a hearth holder and an explorer may feel somewhat contradictory, after all the whole point of the hearth holder is to stay at home while explorers venture far afield. The answer lies in realising that both mindsets are necessary, and the art lies in knowing when and how to access each at the right time for your role.

Meaningful purpose

The healthy and productive expression of all four of these archetypes occurs most powerfully when they are aligned in service of a common purpose. We discussed how to develop greater personal alignment with purpose in Chapter 6, and again in relation to effective teams in Chapter 7. The same principles and practices are relevant for you as a leader. The difference is that as a leader, one of your most important tasks is to establish a shared sense of purpose for your people. As we've already discussed in relation to teams, people thrive when they have a collective sense of purpose and direction.

Your purpose is a believable and compelling answer to **why** your organisation exists. Simon Sinek describes a powerful purpose as a 'just cause' that transcends short term wins and gives long term direction and meaning.[24] And whilst delivering your strategy, being profitable, winning market share or aspiring to be the best you can be are all worthy goals they are not your purpose. To inspire and bring out the best in your team, your purpose should express your team's impact on the lives of the people you serve – whether they are customers, clients, others in your business or society at large.

> **Tony's Chocoloney - "together we will make 100% slave-free the norm in chocolate"**[25]
>
> In 2002 Dutch investigative journalist Teun van de Keuken discovered that all the world's chocolate makers relied on cocoa harvested using child labour. Outraged by the big producer's lack of interest in addressing this illegality, in 2005 he founded his own chocolate company committed to producing 'slave-free' chocolate. Since then, sales have grown, surpassing the big multinational brands in the Netherlands, and spreading throughout Europe and reaching the UK in 2019. In the process, the big chocolate producers have been forced to act with their suppliers to address child labour abuses.

Now, many of you are probably reading this and saying to yourself "having a purpose is all very well when you are in an ethical business trying to save the world, but it is a bit hard to find when we are tucked away in a dark corner running the accounts for a big corporation."

This is the tough reality facing leaders at all levels in many organisations today. It is hard to find a meaningful purpose when your employer is simply interested in making money. Yet one of the major shifts in the 2020s is the recognition that consumers increasingly want to buy from purpose-driven companies, and people increasingly want to work for them.

Reimagining the future

The 2020 COVID pandemic created a once in a generation opportunity to re-imagine how we work.

> *"This is not a time for falling back on comfortable ideology. We need to get off the beaten track, reinvent ourselves, find new ways of living, not least of all me."*
>
> President Emmanuel Macron of France[26]

Reimagining is both daunting and terrifying, energising and overwhelming. It is the epitome of a complex challenge that requires new ways of thinking and working, not simply re-arranging current best practices. Beyond ensuring your company's survival, it is the most important leadership challenge we face.

I encourage you to start within your sphere of influence; whether this is simply yourself, your team, your division or even your whole company. There are four critical areas, and each of the archetypes has an important role to play:

MEANINGFUL PURPOSE (EXPLORER)

What is changing in your context? Are you scanning your horizon to understand the bigger forces at play? Be curious about what's happening in adjacent sectors and other geographies. A useful and well-known framework is a PESTLE analysis. This provides a series of categories, Political, Economic, Social, Technological, Legislative and Environmental. At its most basic level, use these headings to look outside your company and ask, 'what's going on?' A far more powerful level comes when you next ask, 'What's the nature of the relationships between these events?' This helps you appreciate the inter-dependencies of different events and forces. Share your insights, questions and observations with your team and use mind-maps and visual tools to explore connections.

Much as some people would welcome it, there is no return to normal. What does this mean for your personal and organisational purpose? Should or could this change or evolve in a post COVID world? How will your purpose engage your people and customers in the emerging world? Can you articulate it in simple, accessible language? Do you really believe in it, or are you paying lip service?

SUSTAINABLE SUPPLY CHAINS (HEARTH HOLDER)

As I explained at the start of this chapter, responding to the climate emergency is this decade's key challenge. One of the most powerful levers for positive change is for companies to think hard about their whole supply chains. This does not just apply to businesses that create tangible products – this is for service providers too.

Where do your resources come from? How are they transported? If Teun van de Keuken was investigating your business just as he did chocolate manufacturers, would he discover the equivalent of child labour? Could your raw materials be sourced more locally? Where do your products go when they are 'finished? Do they end up in landfill, are they recycled, or can they be re-purposed? What's the real social and environmental impact of your products and services?

HUMAN CENTRED PROCESSES (COACH)

2020 was an unprecedented social experiment. Many millions of people around the world discovered that it is possible to work from home – or indeed anywhere with wi-fi. Of course, many millions also suffered greatly because their work in manufacturing, hospitality or travel absolutely required their physical presence. What have you learned about the adaptability, resourcefulness, and trustworthiness of your people? What does this mean for how your people might work in the future? About how they will travel, where they will work, how will they learn and how they will be rewarded?

EXPERIMENTATION (AGITATOR)

The Agitator has a roving role in each of these domains, to challenge assumptions, hunt down sacred cows, and foster true innovation. Without the Agitator's awkward questions, it will be too easy to fall back into familiar ways of working. The Agitator can encourage safe to fail experiments. These are experiments to find new ways of working within set parameters that ensure that even a 'worst case' outcome is acceptable in terms of financial loss, reputation, or human wellbeing. The Coach is important here too, because people need to be encouraged to understand that they will not be judged on success or failure, but on their capacity to learn and adapt.

Chris's team

We met Chris way back in Chapter 1. Remember he is the CEO of a global engineering firm who's been recruited to lead a major turnaround. One of his first priorities was to ensure he had a competent and well aligned senior leadership team. As well as investing in their development so they had a shared language and ways of working, he also recruited a new COO after he realised that the incumbent did not have access to the necessary worldview to handle the scale of change that was coming.

Let's sit in on a meeting he has called with his senior team to talk about the change ahead. Because the topic is so important the team have chosen to meet in person. Routine and operational meetings usually take place online. The meeting begins by each team member offering a short check in, reporting not on recent tasks that have been achieved, but sharing a few words about how they're feeling and what's relevant in their personal lives at this moment. Each person listens carefully and attends fully to the one who is speaking. Chris goes last, and after sharing his own check in ("...I am feeling a mixture of anticipation and nervousness about this meeting") he segues into the purpose of the meeting:

"I want to share my initial thoughts about the new strategy. You have each contributed your own ideas and I have met many people across the company, but now it's time we talked about it together. I want you all to be forthright, there are no sacred cows as far as I am concerned, and I certainly do not believe I have all the answers myself."

Chris proceeds to talk through a short slide deck, which lays out the key facts and assumptions about the strengths and weaknesses of the company's present position. He is careful to keep his assumptions very clear, and at the end he asks; "I've not been here as long as you guys – what have I missed?" Team members respond candidly, backing up their opinions with short, powerful examples. Chris listens carefully, noticing the occasional spike of irritation when he senses a response that he believes is too conservative. He is well aware that he is strongest when moving into new territory (the explorer) and that he needs to be patient when others are more cautious. He has learned to smile at his own impatience and use it as a cue to listen even more carefully to others.

Chris's team

After an hour or so, the team take a break. Everyone gets up to move and stretch, and few dive straight to their phones. They know it is more important to re-charge and re-fresh for the rest of the meeting than get distracted by email or social media.

When the meeting resumes, Chris starts by framing the next session – explaining that he wants to move to the future and shape a vision for the company five years from now. "I want us to be systematic as we work through this, so I'd like Juan to play the agitator and challenge us hard. Louise, will you take the hearth holder perspective and pay attention to how this works practically. Dave, you are the coach – how will this affect our people? I'll stay in my comfort zone and take explorer."

Despite nominating these roles, as the conversation unfolds team members move fluidly from one archetype to another, like wearing different hats. There is little over-talking, each person is allowed to finish their point before another starts, even if that means moments of silence as people pause to find the right words. From time-to-time Chris intervenes with a question, like "How does this issue relate to the point Louise raised earlier?" and "how might this play out over time?" "Where might this start to become unstable?" These questions deliberately open unexplored perspectives and take the team into new territory.

After an hour or so, a consensus starts to emerge, and Chris summarises and plays it back to the team, checking that everyone has been heard and agrees. He points to the next stage of the process – the team will now pause and reflect on the output for a day or two, then start to move to the next level of detail.

The meeting ends with a round of closing reflections, each person offering an appreciation for a colleague, noting an aspect of the meeting's process that they want to repeat or change next time, or simply sharing how they feel after an intense yet energising three hour working session.

Conclusion

The coming decade will be tough. It started with the COVID pandemic followed by wars in Ukraine and the Middle East that threaten world stability and peace. This decade presents both a crisis and a great opportunity for leaders. We can never fully go back to where we were pre-COVID. Whilst many people may not like being forced to work from home while they look after young children, homeworking will remain an option in the future. Whilst we might hanker after the 'joys' of business travel, we know that it is no longer essential and that virtual meetings can work better than we thought.

Just as well, given that the climate crisis still awaits our full attention. We have all been forced to adapt, and human resilience and ingenuity have enabled us to do so. The leaders and businesses that will thrive will be the ones that re-imagine themselves into the new, emerging future, taking the best of the past but also leaving much behind. These leaders will enable workplaces that are healthy and high performing, adaptable and secure, human focused and technologically agile.

Want to work on this?

Here are three powerful leadership habits to cultivate. Discuss these with a trusted colleague or your coach and choose one that will best help your development right now.

- When I approach a leadership decision, instead of thinking about what's best for me personally I will consider what's best for the whole team or organisation.
- When I approach a problem, instead of defaulting to my preferred leadership archetype, I will explore the issue from the perspective of another archetype.
- When one of my team is lagging, instead of hassling them, I will remind them of their part in our shared purpose.

Want to know more?

I have referenced Simon Sinek's *The infinite game* (Penguin, 2019) several times in this chapter. It's an excellent book that reframes leadership away from the conventional competitive approach, towards long term sustainability.

One of the best guides to understanding and working with polarities is *Navigating polarities, using both/and thinking to lead transformation.* Brian Emerson and Kelly Lewis (Paradoxical Press, 2019). See also Chapter 6 on Opposable thinking in *Upgrade, building your capacity for complexity.* Karen Ellis and Robert Boston (Leaderspace, 2019).

My understanding of systems thinking for leaders is heavily influenced by Alistair Mant. See *Intelligent Leadership.* Alistair Mant (Allen & Unwin, 1997) and for a wonderful extended case study of a real-world leader see *The bastard's a genius – the Robert Clifford story* (Allen & Unwin, 2010).

---

[1] *https://obr.uk/forecasts-in-depth/the-economy-forecast/brexit-analysis/#indepth*
[2] Far reaching ban on single use plastics in England. *https://www.gov.uk/government/news/far-reaching-ban-on-single-use-plastics-in-england*
[3] For example, Oxford University and fossil fuel divestment. *https://www.ox.ac.uk/news-and-events/fossil-fuel-divestment*
[4] Chappet, M.-C. (2022).
[5] Cynefin Framework *https://thecynefin.co/about-us/about-cynefin-framework*
[6] Snowden, D.J., Boone, M.E. (2007)
[7] Mant, A. (1997).

[8] Tree, I. (2019).

[9] Pegg, D. (2020).

[10] Emerson, B and Lewis, K. (2019).

[11] I am far from alone in questioning heroic leadership. See for example The Kings Fund (2011) *The future of leadership and management in the NHS; no more heroes.*

[12] Quick, M. (2018).

[13] Adams. D. (2001).

[14] Perry, C. (2015).

[15] See for example Senge, P. (1990).

[16] Kegan, R., Lahey, L., Fleming, A. and Miller, M. (2014).

[17] Senge, P. (1990).

[18] Shackleton's Ad – Men Wanted for Hazardous Journey, available at *https://discerninghistory.com/2013/05/shackletons-ad-men-wanted-for-hazerdous-journey/*

[19] McCall, T. (2015).

[20] These ideas come Mountford, C. (1973) and more can be read on hunter-gatherers here *https://education.nationalgeographic.org/resource/hunter-gatherer-culture/*

[21] Kraajeijenbrink, K. (2019).

[21] Sinek, S. (2019).

[23] Rand, A. (1996).

[24] Sinek, S. (2019).

[25] Tonys Chocoloney Mission Statement *https://tonyschocolonely.com/us/en/our-mission*

[26] Macron, E (2020) quoted in *The Guardian*, article available at
https://www.theguardian.com/world/2020/apr/13/macron-france-remain-strict-lockdown-for-another-month

Epilogue – the power of having enough, rather than always wanting more

I began this book with a strong critique of the current economic system and the unhealthy, damaging ways of working it engenders. I have sought to provide a 'user guide' that explains why we are as we are; to show that humans are a mess of contradictions; often driven by fear and yet also capable of great love and creativity. In each of the following chapters I have shown how we need to learn how our own motivational needs influence our thoughts, relationships, and actions. Only then can we counter our unhelpful tendencies to objectify others, to narrow our thinking, to scatter our energy or to burnout. Only then can we maintain healthy, effective teams and navigate the many leadership challenges we face. Only then can we create workplaces that allow people to thrive.

The great paradox of modern times is that we all see and feel the need to change yet believe that our individual actions will make no difference. So, we feel powerless and do nothing. We wait for others (the great 'they') to do something first. As indeed they must, for without serious government intervention that legislates for new ways of working, travelling, and using natural resources, we all remain f***ed.

And yet, our society and its economic system grow from the interaction of our many individual lives, as we all seek to meet our needs for acceptance, control, and security. Some are driven by more noble motivations too, a desire to build, create and serve. None of these needs are unique to our time, and indeed motivated the early explorers and merchants who exploited the 'new world' 600 years ago as much as they drive a tech entrepreneur today. The great (evil) genius of capitalism is that it is driven by the human ego's fear of not having enough. This fear leads to greed, the desire to have more. To acquire more, to own more, to use more. No-one is immune to fear or to greed because they come from the same ego that served us as children to seek safety, love and control.[1] Real change, whether as individuals or as society, will come when enough of us learn to move beyond fear and greed and instead focus our creative energy on ensuring there is enough. Enough what? Enough love, enough security, enough control in our individual lives and enough fresh water, healthy food, shelter and meaningful work for the world.

I first encountered Kate Raworth's ideas[2] in 2017 at the annual Meaning Conference in Brighton.[3] She described a vision of a world based on 'enough' – everyone having enough of the basics for life, whilst staying within natural limits and not depleting resources beyond the rate the earth can replenish them. This would be a truly sustainable economy, not one based on endless growth. Kate called this 'doughnut economics' – the inner ring of the doughnut representing the base levels required for healthy life, the outside ring representing the planet's sustainable limits. Fortunately, her work is becoming increasingly influential, and I believe it is a helpful framework for our individual and corporate lives.

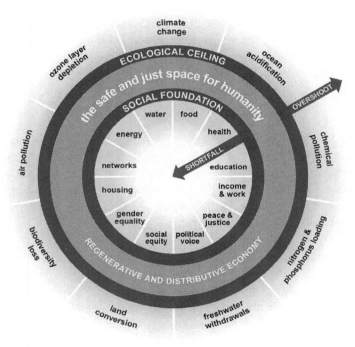

Figure 8 The Doughnut economic model (Raworth)

The great irony is that as individuals, we can learn to appreciate that maybe we *already* have enough. This is the message of the great spiritual traditions; that we suffer from the illusion of separation and lack, instead of recognising our connection and wholeness. We all possess an inner foundation if only we can uncover it. Laura, our workaholic young lawyer, can learn that she is good enough as she is, and that 60 hour working weeks won't make her parents love her more. James, our hard-driven property boss, can discover that even more control in his life won't lead to contentment. Amir can come to appreciate that even if he disagrees with others, his self-worth can remain intact. With self-awareness leading to self-acceptance each of us can let go of the behaviours that lead us to 'overshoot' our personal wellbeing ceiling through overwork or stress. This is the true heart of healthy high performance. The more each of us heals our emotional wounds, and silences that inner voice that whispers "you are not good enough", the more readily we can create healthy workplaces and a just society.

Jonathan Males

---

[1] Although best known for his GROW coaching model, it's worth reading what Sir John Whitmore said about this topic. He saw need and greed as the drivers of the capitalist system as it is, and freedom as the result of a positive evolution. See Whitmore, J. (1997).

[2] For more on Raworth's work on Doughnut Economics
https://www.kateraworth.com/doughnut/

[3] The Meaning conference was held annually until 2019 in Brighton UK bringing together a diverse range of speakers focused on creating more equitable and healthy organisations, *https://meaningconference.co.uk*

Bibliography

- Adams. D. (2001). *The restaurant at the end of the universe.* Pan Macmillan.
- Anthony, S.D. (2016). Kodak's Downfall Wasn't about Technology. [online] *Harvard Business Review.* Available at: https://hbr.org/2016/07/kodaks-downfall-wasnt-about-technology.
- Arbinger Institute (2010). *Leadership and Self-Deception: Getting Out of the Box.* Oakland, CA: Berrett-Koehler Publishers
- Barbalet, J. (2008). *Weber, Passion and Profits: 'The Protestant Ethic and the Spirit of Capitalism' in Context.* Cambridge: Cambridge University Press.
- Bennett, N. and Lemoine, G. J., (2014). *What VUCA really means for you,* available at https://hbr.org/2014/01/what-vuca-really-means-for-you, (accessed 8th March 2023)
- Brower, T. (2023). *Maximize Mental Health With A Few Good Friends: Here's How.* [online] Forbes. Available at: https://www.forbes.com/sites/tracybrower/2023/03/07/maximize-mental-health-with-a-few-good-friends-heres-how/.
- Bungay, S. (2011) *The art of action, how leaders close the gaps between plans, actions and results.* Nicholas Brealey Publishing.
- Chappet, M.-C. (2022). *The incredible downfall of WeWork is about to be a TV miniseries - but what actually happened?* [online] Harper's BAZAAR. Available at: https://www.harpersbazaar.com/uk/culture/culture-news/a38841922/wework-wecrashed-story-explained/.
- Charam, R., Drotter, S., & Noel. J. (2011) *The Leadership Pipeline.* Jossey-Bass.
- Clark, T. (2023). *What is psychological safety? It's a culture of rewarded vulnerability.* https://www.leaderfactor.com/psychological-safety (accessed 09-03-2023)
- Clear, J. (2018). *Atomic Habits,* Random House.
- Cook-Greuter, S. (2004). *Making the Case for a Developmental Perspective.*
- Covey, S.R. (2020). *The seven habits of highly effective people.* Simon and Schuster.
- De Bono, E. (1991). *I am right – you are wrong.* Penguin Books.

- De Visch, J. & Laske, O. (2020). *Practices of dynamic collaboration, a dialogical approach to strengthening collaborative intelligence in teams.* Springer.
- Donahue, J.J. (2020). *Fight-Flight-Freeze System.* In: Zeigler-Hill, V., Shackelford, T.K. (eds) *Encyclopaedia of Personality and Individual Differences.* Springer, Cham. https://doi.org/10.1007/978-3-319-24612-3_751
- Dweck, C. (2016). *Mindset, the New Psychology of Success.* Ballantine Books.
- Edmonson, A. (2023). *Psychological Safety* – Amy C. Edmondson. [online] amycedmondson.com. Available at: https://amycedmondson.com/psychological-safety/.
- Freud, S. (2011). *The Ego and the Id.* United Kingdom: Read Books
- Emerson, B. and Lewis, K. (2019). *Navigating polarities, using both/and thinking to lead transformation.* Paradoxical Press.
- Fritz, R. (1989). *The path of least resistance; learning to become the creative force in your own life.* Fawcett; Rev ed. Edition
- Goleman, D. et al (2001). *Primal Leadership* https://hbr.org/2001/12/primal-leadership-the-hidden-driver-of-great-performance, accessed on 8-03-2023
- Greenfield, S. (2014). *Mind* Change: How Digital Technologies are Leaving Their Mark on Our Brains. United Kingdom: Ebury Publishing
- Harvard Business Review, (2014) *What VUCA really means for you,* available at https://hbr.org/2014/01/what-vuca-really-means-for-you, (accessed 8th March 2023)
- Hawkins, P. (2011). *Leadership team coaching, developing collective transformational leaders.* Kogan Page.
- Heffernan, M. (2009). *Wilful Blindness, why we ignore the obvious at our peril.* Simon and Schuster.
- Hollis, J. (2003). *Finding meaning in the second half of life,* Gotham Books.
- *Institute of Health Equity,* (2020) *The Marmot Review, Ten Years On,* available at https://www.instituteofhealthequity.org/resources-reports/marmot-review-10-years-on (accessed 08-03-2023)
- Kabbat-Zinn, J. (2004). *Wherever you go, there you are; mindfulness meditation for everyday life.* Piatkus.
- Katzenbach, R. & Smith, D. K. (1993). The Discipline of Teams in *Harvard Business Review* Magazine, March–April 1993.

- Kegan, R. & Lahey, L.L. (2009). *Immunity to change*. Harvard Business Press.
- Kegan, R. (1995). *In over our heads, the mental demands of modern life*. Harvard University Press.
- Kegan, R., Lahey, L., Fleming, A. and Miller, M. (2014). Making Business Personal. *Harvard Business Review*. Available at: https://hbr.org/2014/04/making-business-personal. (accessed 08-03-2023)
- King, M L. (1967). *The Three Evils of Society, transcript of Speech given at New Conference of Politics, US*, available at https://www.scribd.com/doc/134362247/Martin-Luther-King-Jr-The-Three-Evils-of-Society-1967#, (accessed on 08/03/23)
- Kraajeijenbrink, K. (2019). *What the 3 Ps of the Triple Bottom Line Really Mean*, article in Forbes, available at https://www.forbes.com/sites/jeroenkraaijenbrink/2019/12/10/what-the-3ps-of-the-triple-bottom-line-really-mean/?sh=d29a6b514359
- Kriegel. R. & Brandt, D. (1997). *Sacred Cows make the best burgers. Developing change-ready people and organizations*. Warner Business Books.
- Kynaston, D. (2020). *Till Time's Last Sand: A History of the Bank of England 1694-2013. United Kingdom: Bloomsbury USA and Lloyds history*, available at https://www.lloyds.com/about-lloyds/history/, (accessed 08/03/23)
- Lunbeck, E. et al, (2019). *Sigmund Freuds the Ego and the Id* available at https://daily.jstor.org/virtual-roundtable-on-the-ego-and-the-id/ (accessed 03-03-2023)
- M. González, V. and Mark, G. (2004). *Constant, Constant, Multi-tasking Craziness, Managing Multiple Working Spheres*. University of California, Irvine, http://www.ics.uci.edu/~gmark/CHI2004.pdf
- Mackey, J. and Sisodia, R. (2013). Conscious Capitalism is not an Oxymoron in *Harvard Business Review*, available at https://hbr.org/2013/01/cultivating-a-higher-conscious (Accessed on 8-03-2023)
- Macleod, S. *Maslow's Hierarchy of Needs Theory*. https://simplypsychology.org/maslow.html (accessed 14/3/23)
- Mant, A. (1997). *Intelligent Leadership*. Allen & Unwin.
- Mason, P. (2016). *Postcapitalism – a guide to our future*. Penguin Books.

- Mattheys, K., Warren, J. and Bambra, C. (2018). '"Treading in sand": A qualitative study of the impact of austerity on inequalities in mental health', *Social Policy & Administration*, 52(7), pp. 1275–1289.
- McCall, T. (2015). How to Innovate with Bimodal IT, Gartner Inc https://www.gartner.com/smarterwithgartner/how-to-innovate-with-bimodal-it
- Mountford, C. (1973). *The Dreamtime: Australian Aboriginal Myths*, Rigby Imprint.
- Nettle, D. (2009). *Personality: What makes you the way you are*, Oxford, Oxford University press.
- Nickerson, R. S. (1998). Confirmation Bias: A Ubiquitous Phenomenon in Many Guises. *Review of General Psychology*, 2(2), 175–220. https://doi.org/10.1037/1089-2680.2.2.175
- Norman, J. (2019). *Adam Smith: What he Thought and Why it Matters*, Penguin Books, London.
- *Our World in Data* (2020), Data on GDP to 2018 from https://ourworldindata.org/grapher/gdp-per-capita-maddison-2020?time=1..latest&country=IDN~ARG~KOR~FRA~GBR~USA~AUT~IND~CHN (Accessed 8/03/23)
- *Our World in Data* (2023), Data on social inequality, available at https://ourworldindata.org/grapher/income-share-of-the-top-10-pip?country=BRA~FRA~CHN~ZAF
- Pegg, D. (2020). Covid-19: did the UK government prepare for the wrong kind of pandemic? *The Guardian*. [online] 21 May. Available at: https://www.theguardian.com/world/2020/may/21/did-the-uk-government-prepare-for-the-wrong-kind-of-pandemic.
- Pendleton, V. (2012). *Between the lines, my autobiography*. Harper Sport.
- Perry, C. (2015). *The Shadow, Article in the Society of Analytic Psychology*, available at, https://www.thesap.org.uk/articles-on-jungian-psychology-2/about-analysis-and-therapy/the-shadow/
- Quick, M. (2018). *Every story in the world has one of these basic plots* BBC culture, available at https://www.bbc.com/culture/article/20180525-every-story-in-the-world-has-one-of-these-six-basic-plots
- Rand, A. (1996). *The fountainhead*. Penguin Random House.
- Richtel, M (2010). quoted in https://www.npr.org/2010/08/24/129384107/digital-overload-your-brain-on-gadgets, Accessed 8-03-2023

- Rock, D. (2009). *Your Brain at Work*, New York, Harper Collins.
- Rooke, D., Fisher, D., Torbert, W. R. (2003). *Personal and Organisational Transformations: Through Action Inquiry.* United Kingdom: Edge/Work.
- Ryan, R. M., Deci, E. L. (2018). Self-Determination Theory: Basic Psychological Needs in *Motivation, Development, and Wellness.* United Kingdom: Guilford Publications.
- Senge, P. (1990). *The fifth discipline, the art and practice of the learning organisation.* Random House.
- Sinek, S. (2019). *The infinite game.* Penguin Random House.
- Smith, A. (1812). *The Theory of Moral Sentiments.* United Kingdom: (n.p.).
- Smith, A. (1776). *An Inquiry into the Nature and Causes of the Wealth of Nations.* United Kingdom: Strahan.
- Smith, M. (1998). Commuter Suffers Signal Failure on 8am to Waterloo, *Daily Telegraph*, 10 December 1998, page 7.
- Snowden, D.J., Boone, M.E.(2007) A Leader's Framework for Decision Making, *Harvard Business Review*, November 2007.
- Spira, J B. & Feintuch, J B. (2005). *The Cost of Not Paying Attention: How Interruptions Impact Knowledge Worker Productivity.* Basex.
- Sternberg, R.J, Grigorenko, E.L. (2004). *Intelligence and culture: how culture shapes what intelligence means, and the implications for a science of well-being.*
- Syer, J. & Connolly, C. (1996). *How teamwork works, the dynamics of effective team development.* McGraw Hill.
- Syer, J. (1986). *Team Spirit, the elusive experience.* Sportspages.
- Torbert, W. R. (2004). *Action Inquiry: The Secret of Timely and Transforming Leadership.* Berrett-Koehler Publishers.
- Tree, I. (2019). *Wilding – the return of nature to a British farm.* Picador.
- Tutino, J. (2017). *Slavery and Historical Capitalism During the Nineteenth Century.* United States: Lexington Books.
- Van Oech, R. (2008). *A Whack on the Side of the Head; How You Can Be More Creative.* Grand Central Publishing.
- Warner, C. T. (2016). *Bonds That Make Us Free: Healing Our Relationships, Coming to Ourselves.* United States: Shadow Mountain.
- Weber, M. (2012). *The Protestant Ethic and the Spirit of Capitalism.* United States: Dover Publications.
- Weeks, K. (2019). Every generation wants meaningful work, *Harvard Business Review*, 2019, available at https://hbr.org/2017/07/every-

generation-wants-meaningful-work-but-thinks-other-age-groups-are-in-it-for-the-money?, (accessed 03-03-2023)

- Weir, K. (2014). *The Lasting Impact of Neglect* available at https://www.apa.org/monitor/2014/06/neglect (Accessed 03-03-2023)
- Whitmore, J. (1997). *Need, greed or freedom; business changes and personal choices.* Element Books Limited.
- Whyte, D. (2012). *Start Close In. River Flow: New & Selected Poems.* Many Rivers Press.
- Xu, X., Mishra, G.D., Holt-Lunstad, J. and Jones, M. (2023). Social relationship satisfaction and accumulation of chronic conditions and multimorbidity: a national cohort of Australian women. General Psychiatry, 36(1), p.e100925. doi:https://doi.org/10.1136/gpsych-2022-100925.